ISNHCP Natural Trim Training Manual
Basic Guidelines

Institute for the Study of
Natural Horse Care Practices

Natural Trim
Training Manual

Basic Guidelines

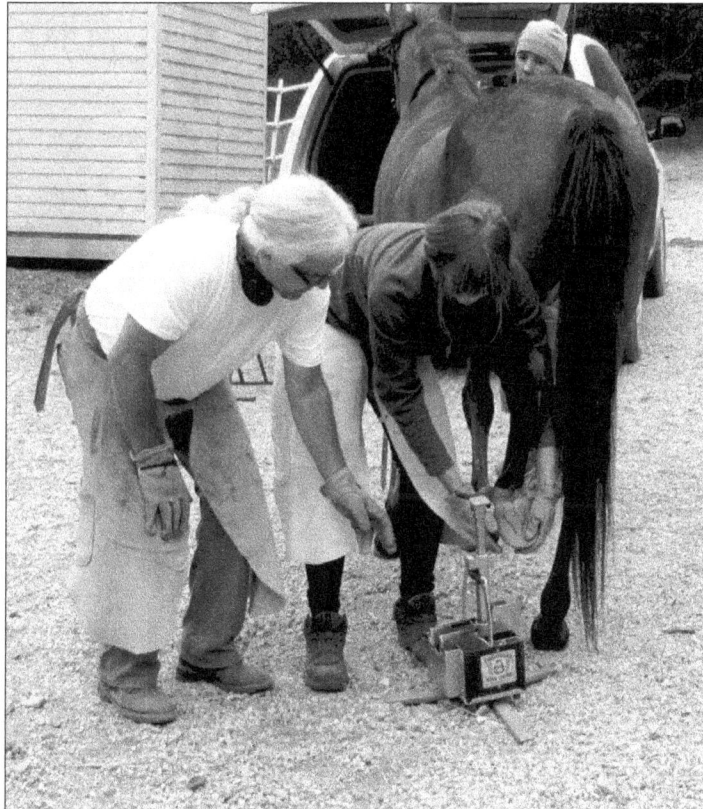

Jaime Jackson

A Publication of the ISNHCP

Book designed by the author.
Published for the ISNHCP by J. Jackson Publishing

For further information:

J. Jackson Publishing
PO Box 1765
Harrison, AR 72602-1765

info@isnhcp.net
www.ISNHCP.net

ISBN: 978-1-7355358-0-7 (2020 edition)
ISBN: 978-0-9848399-5-7 (2017 edition)

The natural hoof care guidelines described in this training manual are intended by the author Jaime Jackson and the ISNHCP, to be conducted under the supervision of authorized ISNHCP clinicians and field instructors in keeping with the instructional protocols of the ISNHCP Natural Trim Training Program as presented and explained in this training manual and on the ISNHCP Natural Trim website (www.ISNHCP. net). Natural hoof care is a sophisticated and highly technical process that should only be practiced by qualified natural hoof care practitioners trained and ideally certified in the principles and practices described in these guidelines, or by persons under their immediate supervision. Thus, neither the ISNHCP, the author, nor J. Jackson Publishing, accept responsibility for the applications or misapplications of these guidelines.

Contents

Student taking the 3rd Position in Sequencing.

Introduction

This "Basic" *Natural Trim Training Program* is a comprehensive, academic, and hands-on foundational course in the artful science of natural hoof care (NHC). The natural trim is defined as a *humane, barefoot trimming method that mimics the natural wear patterns of wild, free-roaming horses* (aka, the "mustang") of the U.S. Great Basin. This action immediately "triggers" healthy growth patterns, that, when accompanied by other natural holistic practices also based on the wild horse model, eventually result in naturally shaped hooves. By all accounts, this transformation is truly a miracle of nature, but, technically, it is an outcome of the specie's adaptation, embedded in the DNA of every living horse today. It is of paramount importance to recognize that NHC practitioners do not force the foot to look a certain way (e.g., like a wild horse hoof), but facilitate its growth through the natural trim method of mimicking wild horse hoof wear patterns.

Basic Natural Trim Guidelines

This training program teaches the *Basic Natural Trim* Guidelines. The Basic Guidelines are useful for horses that are not suffering from extreme hoof deformities. For those rare instances of extreme deformity, the Advanced Guidelines are deployed (discussed shortly).

4 Pillars of NHC

A distinction is made between the terms "natural trim" and "natural hoof care." The natural trim refers specifically to trim mechanics — how one actually trims the hoof. Natural hoof care casts the natural trim in a much bigger context. This is referred to in our discipline as the *Four Pillars of natural horse care (NHC)*. These pillars are the foundations of natural horse care based on the wild horse model. They include *natural boarding, natural horsemanship, a reasonably natural diet, and the natural trim.* Years of experience have shown us that it is virtually impossible to conduct a natural trim consistently with full import without any regard to the other three pillars.

As an example, a horse fed a diet that causes inflammation inside the horse's foot (such as laminitis), resulting in degradation of the outer hoof, will continue to do so regardless of the practitioner's diligence in carrying out natural trim mechanics. Likewise a horse that is ridden without any concern for or knowledge of how the species moves naturally, can not only damage the horse's upper body, but also alter hoof growth patterns (such as Navicular Syndrome). The natural trim, on its own, cannot prevent or help in the remediation of these problems without intervention by the other three pillars. Thus, in our discipline, natural hoof care equates specifically to the 4 Pillars of NHC. For this reason, students are educated about all four Pillars so as to enhance their effectiveness as trimmer.

Advanced Natural Trim Guidelines

Here another important distinction is made between the Basic and Advanced Natural Trim Guidelines. The *Basic Guidelines* taught in this training program emphasize hooves not complicated by *extreme capsule deformity.** Many years of experience have shown the ISNHCP leadership that such deformity — typically the outcome of criminal neglect, harmful hoof care methods, and diets that cause severe pathological migrations of hoof mass — only create confusion in the minds of beginning students. The "basics" of natural trim mechanics become mired and lost in the overwhelming complications of dealing with severely troubled hooves.

The ISNHCP recognizes that until basic natural trim mechanics are clearly understood and mastered on hooves suffering minimal deformity, the path to resolving the complexities of extreme deformity is virtually untenable. One must "learn to crawl before one learns to walk." Indeed, to tackle the worst deformed hooves imaginable, the trimmer must not only be sound in the basics, but be academically prepared as well. Further, the ISNHCP holds that such hooves should be undertaken within a veterinary context due to the possibilities of internal damage, infection, the need for radiology and other higher technologies, the need to remove the horse from the owner (legally or otherwise for rehabilitation), mental damage caused to the horse, and for legal protection of the practitioner (if not a vet) wherever barefoot hoof care has not been sanctioned by governments. This is not to say that the Advanced Guidelines constitute a veterinary procedure in themselves — they do not when done correctly — only that the animal is best served when they are deployed as an adjunct to veterinary intervention as explained above.

Origins of the Basic Natural Trim Guidelines

The official ISNHCP trimming guidelines are based on the wild horse research conducted by myself in the 1980s in the U.S. Great Basin, followed by many years of experimentation culminating in a proven method. When properly adhered to, these guidelines will serve to prevent mistakes that harm the horse and the hooves, while facilitating naturally shaped hooves within the context of the 4 Pillars of NHC.

The ISNHCP Website

The ISNHCP website (www.ISNHCP.net) is the "official" headquarters of

*Capsule is commonly used in place of hoof, referring specifically to the tough outer protective shell of the foot. Thus, the horse's foot includes the outer capsule *and* all of its contents.

Jaime Jackson base camp in central Nevada, U.S. Great Basin, c. early 1984. (AANHCP Archives)

the Basic Natural Trim ISNHCP Training Program. Official training requirements are posted there, and students are required to go there to find their way through the training program. Besides the training steps, there is information posted on required tools and equipment, recommended membership in student support/study groups, list of our clinicians and links to their training dates, and more. Visit the website often during your training to keep tabs on possible changes in the training steps.

ISNHCP Student Facebook Page

The ISNHCP Student Facebook Page is a private page created and administered by the ISNHCP. It is for students in training who wish to connect, share news, and also get updates from ISNHCP administrators. This page, however, is not created for instructional purposes, which is the function of the training program. Most students appear to visit this page daily.

ISNHCP Student Study/Support Groups

All ISNHCP students are required to join a support group. Query others on the Student Facebook page to join an existing one or create a new one, or request assignment to one by contacting the ISNHCP. The purpose of the support groups is to provide peer based study time together as they choose, obtain clarification of the training program from the SG host or fellow members, and -- where possible -- come together vis a vis to practice what they are being taught in a clinic type environment. The support groups are not run by the ISNHCP, nor by our clinicians and Field Instructors, but by the students themselves insulated from all but themselves.

The Training Steps

As explained on the ISNHCP website, this training program includes both academic and hands-on instruction. This includes quizzes intended to be used by you as learning aids, submitted written exams enabling the ISNHCP to evaluate your understanding of required subject matter, and a continuous stream of field evaluations of performance by our clinicians and field instructors throughout the course of your training. Students must demonstrate evidence of competency at each stage of their training if they are to proceed to the next step. All along the way, training reports are filed by your teachers with the ISNHCP for review and placement in your training file where it is held in confidence.

The ISNHCP authorizes students to proceed with training from one step to the next, or to return to previous steps for *remediation*, based on training reports. This system of accountability protects horses and you. Our goal is to produce competent, professional level hoof care practitioners who represent the ISNHCP's vital mission in the field.

Primary Purpose of this Training Manual

Beyond this Introduction, the purpose of this training manual is to guide you through Step 1 — Independent Study. There is much learning material for you to go through with diligence, the purpose of which is to prepare you for your hand's-on training, Step 1 Quiz, Final Written and Field Exams, and an academic understanding of NHC. The more you bolster your understanding of NHC principles, the more you will get out of your training in the field. Your library of educational materials is something you can return to again and again during training, and even after you've graduated. If you want to be the best practitioner you can be, then Step 1 is the foundation you will need to build upon.

The following course text books include a brief of each book followed by a True/False quiz. The purpose of the quizzes is to aid you in understanding the material, which will help you to develop a working language of NHC. This will enable you to speak and communicate in our language with other ISNHCP students and practitioners. It will also make you more effective in explaining NHC to your clients. *Instructions: Before taking the quiz, first write down your answers; then go to the quiz key at the back of the Training Manual and compare your answers. If you missed the question, use the key to take you to the correct page in the book and study that section. If you don't understand the answer take your question/s into your support group to get help figuring it out.*

Step 1 Independent Study
Reading Assignments & Quizzes

The Natural Horse
Lessons From the Wild

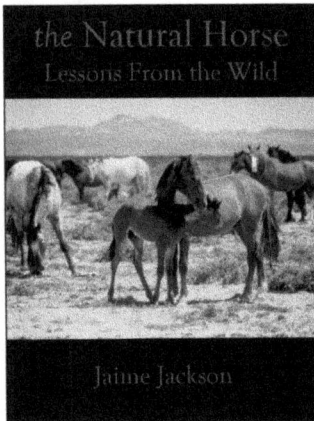

The Natural Horse: Lessons From the Wild (2020 edition) is the foundational work not only for the ISNHCP Natural Trim Training Program, but for all four of the NHC Pillars as explained on the back cover of the book. The 2020 edition is a update of the 1992 edition.

This book should be studied closely from front to back. There is new information in it, and clarification of things written in the first edition. NHC as we know it today, did not exist before the book was published, and for many years after. The application of the wild horse model to horses living in captivity (domestication) had to be tested and proven. As a model, it was unheard of across all but a few pockets of the international horse using community. There was such little interest in the first edition that it was abandoned by Northland Publishing just three years after being released. In fact, before 1996 had arrived, *The Natural Horse* had gone out of print. Worse, no other publishers were interested in taking it over. The NHC movement based on this model might have ended then had it not been for the arrival of personal computers and the Internet.

In 2000, a group of unrelated horse owners living across the U.S. contacted me around the same time to talk about the possibility of forming a new organization to promote natural hoof care based on my research. I agreed with certain provisions: that they meet with me in Harrison, Arkansas, and that we trim together to confirm we were on the same page. All agreed, and the American Association of Natural Hoof Care Practitioners (AANHCP) was soon formed. By 2004, the name was changed to Association for the Advancement of Natural Hoof Care Practices, recognizing that interest and membership were no longer exclusively "American." As more years went by, "Natural Hoof Care" changed to "Natural Horse Care," reflecting the holistic premise of the wild horse model being more than just hooves. Ironically, interest and focus on the book that started it all waned and gave way to other books more geared to trimming horses. Some considered the book too "esoteric," even deeming it irrelevant.

By 2009, a new generation of members had arrived and renewed focus was given to *The Natural Horse* and other books less related to trimming horses, including *Paddock Paradise* and *Laminitis: A Plague*. At this time, training was moved from the AANHCP to the ISNHCP. This transition arguably saved *The Natural Horse* from a second possibility of demise. But it has survived and since returned to its rightful position at the center of NHC.

6

The Natural Horse Quiz* (All T/F)

1. With the help of the BLM, Jackson studied two samples of 125 Great Basin wild horses, totaling 1,000 sets of front/hind hooves.

2. The facility where I measured most of the hooves of captured horses is known as the Litchfield Corrals, located twenty miles east of Susanville, California.

3. When I wrote *The Natural Horse* in the late 1980s I was still a farrier.

4. America's wild horses are feral horses, the offspring of domestic horses that have been turned loose, or escaped, into the wild.

5. Some time around 7,000 B.C. (late Pleistocene Epoch, "Ice Age"), the wild horse along with many other large land mammals, including the mammoth, mastodon, and sabertooth tiger, vanished from the North American continent. Not until 9,000 years later were they first reintroduced by Spanish conquistadores.

6. By the early 1800s, eyewitnesses estimated America's wild horse population at 2 to 5 million.

7. Not long before I entered wild horse country in 1982, no more than 50,000 wild horses were left on the open ranges due to the encroachments of civilization. Congress had passed two laws to protect wild horses from total eradication. Public Law 86-234, also known as the Wild Horse Annie Act — named after Velma Johnston, one of its principal supporters — passed in 1959. It prohibited the capture or destruction of wild horses using inhumane methods. Public Law 92-195, the Wild, Free-Roaming Horse and Burro Act, was passed in 1971; this put all wild horses under the administration of the U.S. Bureau of Land Management (BLM).

8. According to a BLM public affairs official, "Calvary mounts, work horses and escaped or abandoned saddle animals from many breeds have all contributed to the wild horse's lineage . . . only a few descended from Spanish blood."

9. To be perfectly clear, the mustang, *Equus caballus*, *Equus ferus caballus*, and *Equus ferus ferus* are the same species and are genetically indistinguishable from each other. Only lifestyle and environment distinguish the horse living in the wild from the one living in human captivity.

10. Most horse families are composed of a single dominant stallion, the *monarch*, and a closely guarded *harem* of females with whom he bonds and breeds.

11. Great Basin lands that are home to its wild horses are similar. Typically, there are mountains (5,000 to 10,000 feet), small buttes (mesas), gently rolling hills, and broad alluvial plains. Rocks and boulders are scattered everywhere. The plains, where natural, are normally a mixture of firm soil and soft sand, interspersed with small volcanic rocks and a myriad of plant life and grasses.

12. *Home range* can be defined as any area where a band, or assembly of related bands, happens to take up residence in order to exact their survival needs. The size and shape of the home range is not fixed, as though an invisible fence were in place.

13. Wild horse territorial behavior is exhibited by the presence of "stud piles" — fairly large piles of dung, some as high as two to three feet — excreted by various bands occupying the same rangeland.

*Quiz key is appended at the back of the book.

Study hints: Quizzes with answer keys are an excellent way to learn and confirm one's understanding. As study guides, I rarely blend questions coming from different chapters. I believe it is more useful to keep them sequential by chapter with very few exceptions. To get the most out of these, first do the reading. Then take the quiz. Write down your answers before you go to the key! So as to be honest with yourself, mark your answers as T, F, or ? (meaning you're not sure or don't know. Going to the key first will just confirm what you don't know — and you won't learn a thing! To learn, the brain must work and process information to understand; it is also very good at "just looking," another path to learning nothing!

14. The basic elements of the *natural gait complex* — the hereditary locomotive archetype of *Equus ferus caballus** — results from specific behaviors that are routine and uniform across all of wild horse society.

15. *Collection* is essentially a centering or balancing process that is natural to the horse.

16. We should try to understand the mechanics of natural movement within the context of the behaviors that produce it so uniformly across wild horse society.

17. The hooves of the horse are like little mirrors that reflect back upon the animal's entire locomotive experience. In this way, they are visible, tangible repositories of knowledge of lifestyle.

18. The *Natural Gait Complex* refers specifically to the horse's *footfall sequences, leads, stride and stride extension, rhythm, tempo, cadence, and suspension.*

19. The leading or initiating hind leg is pivotal in many ways to the natural locomotion of the horse. Not only does it mark the first step, or footfall, of a stride . . . but it is the leg upon which the horse initiates changes in lead, direction of travel, body extension or contraction, gait, tempo, speed, and collection.

20. *Collection* represents a distinct change in the temperament, poise, body posture, and locomotive style of the horse from the ordinary to the extraordinary.

21. The corollary between altering stride extension and cadence amid constant tempo and rhythm — resulting in changes in speed — has been an important focus among many of the world's finest riders and trainers.

22. Xenophon wrote that collection is not something that can be forced upon the horse. It is a state of mind and body in which the horse engages willfully due to specific behavioral stimuli.

23. Collection is innate to the animal, who knows when, where, to what extent, and how to collect themselves.

24. The natural hoof is uniform in terms of its fundamental front and hind shapes throughout wild horse society, but it is also uniquely endowed with endless subtle variations in angle, size, and color (pigmentation or absence of) that set the hooves of one horse off from those of another.

25. Averages and ranges are included for a few of the dozen or so measurement categories I sampled. Hind hooves, on average, are slightly smaller than front hooves.

26. Not surprising, overall hoof size increased directly with a horse's age until about age five.

27. Basically, I found three hoof color schemes: yellowish to whitish light-colored hooves lacking pigmentation; striated and mottled hooves with various combinations of black pigmentation and no pigmentation; and all black pigmented hooves.

28. The angle of growth of the hoof wall is steeper at the toe than at the heel — the grain is not parallel from toe to heel.

29. The term *wall bevel*, in spite of its common usage among farriers and some horse enthusiasts, is probably misleading.

30. Although I examined hooves in both winter and summer, it was never clear whether frogs underwent a molting process or were kept constantly trim as a re-

sult of locomotive wear.

31. The frog, frog stay, and digital cushion serve to help brace the hoof during support while mitigating associated concussional shock waves coming upwards from ground impact.

32. The volar profile — the bottom of the hoof — is recessed in distinct gradations from one structure to the next.

33. I found that two hooves with the same heel length and identical toe lengths could have entirely different toe angles.

34. *Hoof symmetry* refers to the correspondence in size, form, and arrangement of structures or parts of the hoof on opposite sides of the hoof's *median plane*.

35. The NHC hoof mechanism is a simplified model that explains the naturally balanced hoof's changes as it passes through its flight and support phases.

36. Areas of active and passive wear are not carved into the hoof by the natural hoof care practitioner — they emerge and recede respectively as a consequence of natural movement.

37. Little is known radiographically about the wild horse hoof.

38. Heel growth naturally occurs at a slower rate than at the toe.

39. P3 is a non-weight bearing structure.

40. Nature selects for a broad range of physical and temperamental types, all of which appear to be perfectly suitable for a rugged life in the wild. Variation is clearly nature's way.

41. The principal idea behind generating naturally shaped hooves in the domestic horse is simple: to help the animal move in the way that nature intended.

42. Hoof measurements are arguably the most important part of the natural trim method, which is why we call them the *Critical Measurements*.

43. The HMR uses the SP (support plane) to determine the hoof's VP (volar plane).

44. *Nipper dragging* is a unique technique for removing excess sole growth.

45. The sole dermis (growth corium) extrudes layer upon layer of sheets of epidermis called *solar plates*.

46. Nipper "runs" commence at the toe because starting at the heels runs the risk of unbalancing the heel buttresses.

47. A distinct widening of the medial toe wall typically corresponds to a natural *support pillar*.

48. The midline of the volar profile is technically known in NHC as the *Medial Axis of the Volar Profile* ("MAVP").

49. The *Mediolateral Heel Axis* ("MLHA") is used when sighting the back of the hoof to balance the heels.

50. The Mustang Roll technically is a biodynamic growth pattern that we facilitate through precision trimming and natural boarding.

51. Setting the nipper blade at the juncture of the *s. medium* with the *s. internum* facilitates the most important cut of the Mustang Roll.

52. The Mustang Roll includes all the strata of the hoof wall and the *s. lamellatum*.

53. Also critical the Mustang Roll is that the nipper cut leave the *s. lamellatum* active (distal) to the contiguous sole, but passive (proximal) to the *s. internum*.

54. There are no accessible "flat" surfaces in the naturally shaped volar profile to rasp.

55. The natural biodynamic response of the Mustang Roll includes a rim of protruding *s. internum* that extends to the entire distal periphery of the capsule, including the heel buttresses and the bars whose turns form the seats-of-corn.

56. Excess growth, in the NHC interpretation, is actually different than what is commonly referred to as "flare." *Flare* is a common, but unnatural, growth pattern seen in domesticated horse populations today. It is characterized by a weakened hoof wall that typically "bends" outwards.

57. The wear line is the upper extent of the roll on the outer wall, and is very distinct in the wild horse hoof.

58. "Walking the hoof stand" means encircling the hoof while it is stabilized on the grip head of the hoof stand.

59. Bringing the outermost edge of the *s. internum* just into view is a critical step in pre-forming the Mustang Roll.

60. The trimmer's "deep and low" stance works well with the horse's anatomy, and the animal readily accommodates it.

61. The HB-1 (Hoof Buffer) is the final tool used to complete the natural trim.

62. The outer layers of the frog separate from the hoof in a similar way that solar plates leave the sole.

63. The *Hoof Balancer Tool* is used in two ways: 1) As a sighting instrument for balancing the heels; 2) As an overlay upon the volar profile of the hoof for determining the location of the support triad.

64. The 5 Basic Positions of Sequencing taught in the ISNHCP Natural Trim Training Program are an amalgamation of techniques I learned many years ago as a farrier, what I learned from wild and domesticated horses, innovations that coincided with the development of new tools and equipment, and the requirements of the natural trim itself to do it correctly in keeping with the wild horse model.

65. Sequencing involves all parts of the trimming process except the trim itself.

66. "Paddock Paradise" is a concept for natural horse boarding borne of the wild horse lifestyle in the U.S. Great Basin.

67. Technically, laminitis occurs as a pathological separation of the hoof from the horse.

68. *Lamina* or *laminae* (plural) refers to the network of dermal and epidermal leaf-like structures that interlock together (called "interdigitation") to form a complex bridge of connective tissue between the inner hoof wall and the outer face of the lowermost bone of the horse's foot. Collectively, these laminae form the *s. lamellatum.*

69. Laminitis is not limited to the laminae of the hoof, for separation of the hoof from the horse also occurs across the sole, frog, or wherever the hoof might be attached to the horse's foot.

70. The *laminitis zone* is technically referred to as the *lamellar attachment mechanism*

("LAM"). It is here that laminitis occurs.

71. The *basement membrane* is a thin membranous sheet of tough connective tissue

72. When we apply the principles and proven practices of *natural horse care* ("NHC") based on the wild, free-roaming horse of the Great Basin, healing — and preventing — laminitis is facilitated through basic and relatively straightforward changes in how we manage our horses.

The Natural Trim
Basic Guidelines

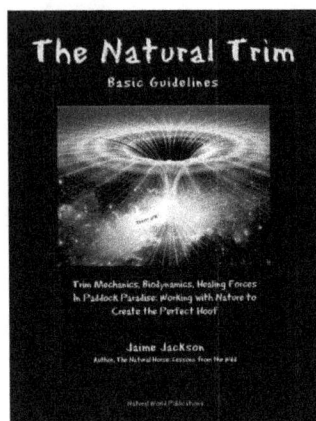

The Natural Trim: Basic Guidelines (2019 edition) is the new foundational work introducing students to the natural trim. Its immediate ancestor is *The Natural Trim: Principles and Practice* (2012, rev. 2019), which still serves this training program, however. Understanding the difference between the two is important and explains why *Principles and Practice* has not been discontinued altogether.

The *Basic Guidelines*, as we call them, were born of new things I learned about the natural trim during the eight years I trimmed our horses at the AANHCP Paddock Paradise facility in Lompoc. These are revealed in the text book, and they will be drawn to your attention as you read and study the book in this section of the training manual. In writing the Basic Guidelines, it also became necessary to alter the language of NHC to some extent. This meant replacing more lay terminology for anatomical structures with identifiers that are used in veterinary science textbooks. But only to the extent I felt it necessary to equip our students with a better understanding of the hoof. There is much that is written about the horse's foot in the scientific literature that conflicts with the wild horse model, and for this reason it serves no good purpose to use it and confuse our students. Finally, it also became clear to me the necessity of purging as many references to pathology as possible. The reason is the recognition that what is needed is a separate text *and* training program to deal with the complexities of deformed hooves and sick horses. One specifically conducted within a sanctioned and fully supported veterinary context. Discussions for creating such a program with our ISNHCP veterinarians is underway.

Principles and Practice was written early in the Paddock Paradise experiment, and its full impact on the horse's hooves was not yet fully understood. This book was revised in 2019 to include information about Paddock Paradise, but the decision was made to not restructure the entire book to integrate the new trimming insights. Regardless, a wealth of information related to the natural trim still existed in the book to keep it alive, without burdening the *Basic Guidelines* with it. This pattern of evolution in my writing about the natural trim dates back many generations to the early 1990's. First tucked within the earliest edition of *The Natural horse*; next the first stand-alone trimming text, *Horse Owners Guide to Natural Hoof Care*; then several editions of *Principles and Practice*; and, finally, the *Basic Guidelines*. Arguably, there will be new texts, written by others, long after I've left the planet.

Basic Guidelines Quiz

1. Unnatural lifestyles create unnaturally shaped hooves, no matter how precise the natural trim.

2. In 2010, fate provided me with the opportunity to create a Paddock Paradise, replete with horses trimmed only by me. The natural trim would be put to the test and I would see the results before my very eyes.

3. It became unmistakably clear to me that it was the "wildness" of our horses' hooves that left the indelible impression of consternation on visitors' faces.

4. I have come to realize that wildness can be a formidable barrier to understanding transformative events in the conscious mind that is saturated with, and only knows, domestication.

5. Paddock Paradise, as I had hoped, breeched the barrier between wildness and domestication. But, in so doing, created a new abstraction, a void fraught with a steady stream of blank human faces.

6. The natural trim, in my mind, had, in fact, metamorphosed from basic trim mechanics into a "chess game" of complex biodynamic responses to what I did to the hoof. If I did such and such, what would the response be?

7. The hoof is biologically equipped to work with us, or fail in the worst of ways.

8. One does not force the foot to look like a wild horse hoof, but simply facilitates its growth through the natural trim method.

9. We use the wild horse hoof as our model simply because both the wild horse and their hooves are the pictures of equine health and soundness.

10. I still find it hard to believe that, until I conducted my wild horse research literally thousands of years after the first horse was domesticated, the scientific basis for the "natural trim" has been both unpublished and unknown.

11. My wild horse hoof research findings were first presented in 1988 at the Annual Conference of the American Farriers Association in Lexington, Kentucky (USA).

12. The Basic Guidelines are used when hooves are healthy and not suffering from extreme deformity due to chronic laminitis, criminal neglect, and hoof care methods which force the hoof into unnatural, if not pathological, shapes and sizes.

13. The evolutionary descent of *E. ferus caballus* through natural selection brings with it a powerful, although unseen, force embedded in the animal's DNA. In NHC science, we call this the adaptation force (or simply the A-force).

14. It is entirely plausible that Global Warming caused a retreat of glaciers in the late Pleistocene Epoch that spawned sugar-rich grasses in their wake that many ungulates (hoofed animals) including the horse could not digest. This metabolic incapacitation led to unprecedented levels of a debilitating and life-threatening disease NHC science defines as Whole Horse Inflammatory Disease (WHID).

15. WHID expresses itself symptomatically throughout the horse's body as a range of bodily disorders, such as colic, abnormal hair growth, cancer, organ failure, inflammation of the feet resulting in lameness.

16. I had presented 30 freeze-dried wild horse hoof biospecimens at the 1988 American Farriers Association Annual Conference. All who came by my table agreed: the hooves were peculiar looking, were not balanced, and badly needed correc-

tion!

17. Today, trained NHC practitioners like myself understand that the range of outcomes produced by the natural trim correspond directly with the faithfulness with which horse owners embrace and act upon the other 3 Pillars.

Note: Pages 18-25 were introduced to you in *The Natural Horse*. This is incredibly important information to go through carefully as it is foundational to the Navigational Landmarks from which the Critical Measurements are derived. It may be helpful to return to *The Natural Horse* and contrast the discussions.

18. A deeper knowledge of the structures of the horse's foot and related biology really only comes into play when tackling the problems associated with upper body trauma and diseases resulting in extreme capsule deformity.

19. An important distinction should be made between the oft heard terms "hoof, capsule, and foot." Hoof and capsule are synonymous. They correspond to the outer or epidermal parts (epidermis : outer skin that lacks nerves and blood vessels) of the horse's foot that we can see and touch. The horse's "foot," in contrast, refers to all of the epidermal parts and its contents.

20. The parts of the capsule are *biodynamic*, meaning they are capable of changing their location, mass, and angle of growth.

21. The outer hoof wall is comprised of the toe, quarter, and heel; these artificial divisions are only approximations.

22. As a farrier, I was taught that the toe wall and the heel both grow at the same angle; this is an entrenched farrier mythology disproved by the wild horse model.

23. The wear line of the Mustang Roll circumscribes the entire hoof wall, approximately 1 cm above ground level (i.e., the Support Plane, "SP").

24. The epidermal structures of the foot's volar profile include the ground-bearing surface of the hoof wall, sole, and frog.

25. The *hard sole plane* (HSP) is virtually unseen and, therefore, unknown in domestication because, unlike in the wild or in a PP that simulates that adaptive environment, it is invariably removed by excessively trimming or shrouded in excess growth (i.e., solar plates).

26. The tendency, if not the practice, of hoof care professionals is to trim the frog until its "flaps" are removed. This constitutes a violation of the Basic Guidelines because, as the wild horse model reveals here, the flaps are intended to be there, in tact, as part of the hoof's epidermal armor.

27. The *digital cushion* is a fibro-fatty structure lying above (proximal to) the frog. Its posterior salience blends with the subcutaneous tissues of the skin and periople to form the heel bulbs. The frog provides epidermal armor for the digital cushion.

28. *The s. tectorium, s. medium, s. internum,* and *s. lamellatum* collectively form the Mustang Roll.

29. The bones of the horse's <u>foot</u> include the cannon bone, splint bones, sessamoid bones, long and short pastern bones, coffin bone, and the navicular bone.

30. While there is considerable emphasis placed on the alignment of the bones of the digit (P1, P2, and P3) among farriers, vets, and even generic (don't follow the wild horse model) barefoot trimmers, this is of little or no interest to the NHC practitioner who simply trims the hoof.

31. There are two major tendons acting upon the horse's foot, the deep digital flexor tendon (DDFT) and the common digital extensor tendon (CDET).

32. The actions of the DDFT and CDET upon the bones and joints are complex as the foot moves through its support and flight phases (recall Table 3-4 in *The Natural Horse*). While interesting from a biomechanical standpoint, they are not germane to the natural trim, which, by definition, facilitates the natural actions of all these structures, whatever they might be, by default.

[Note to student: from page 36 to page 43 addresses the birth of the capsule. This is an extremely important part of your education and is deserved of much time and study.]

33. While one can distinguish the hoof wall corium from the sole corium, frog corium, and other coria, NHC science treats all the foot's coria as a single, integrated body called the Supercorium.

34. If [the hoof is] not shod or subjected to unnatural management practices, all epidermal armor manufactured by the Supercorium is subject to natural and well-orchestrated mass changes that may occur simultaneously anywhere at any time across the entire hoof . . . such changes operate outside current published farriery and veterinary models of the shod hoof.

35. In effect, the hoof wall is actually hair cemented together.

36. I believe the rise of "corrective shoeing" can be attributed to unresponsive pathological hoof growth patterns.

37. Like other coria of the Supercorium, the sole corium is highly vascularized and contributes to intracapsular hydraulic forces of the hoof mechanism.

38. While the sole and frog support weight-bearing forces, it is also true that, relative to SP, those same weight-bearing forces are going to concentrate more over the hoof wall because — in the naturally shaped hoof — neither the sole nor the frog endure direct contact with SP.

39. Close examination reveals that only one stratum of the hoof wall makes contact with SP: the *s. internum* . . . . One could argue, of course, that, in life, the entire bottom of the hoof endures ground contact. True! But, the fact remains, weight-bearing forces always seek out the most immediate path to the ground.

40. Relative concavity is as follows across the volar profile, beginning with the Mustang Roll: *s. tectorium* is proximal to *s. medium*, which is proximal to *s. internum*, which is distal to the *s. lamellatum*, which is distal to the sole, which is distal to the frog.

41. H° is important because it tells us about the stability or instability of the hoof relative to its natural state (N°).

42. Hooves suffering from unnatural care practices will reveal shifts in H° — called migrations — away from the natural ranges for N°.

43. H° exists in a mysterious tug of war between its ancestral A-force and the contemporaneous effects of domestication.

44. Knowing where H° is going, and why, is our challenge as NHC practitioners. Our goal is for H° to settle, accompanied by the soundness and vitality of the horse.

45. The *Critical Measurements* are important because they are based on the theory of H° — and, thus, connect us directly to the wild horse model — and because they guide us safely through the natural trim by enabling "safe cuts" to the millimeter and single degree accuracy.

46. The Support Plane (SP) is any level surface that can support the horse's hoof; the Volar Plane (VP) corresponds to the points of the hoof wall pressing against the SP.

47. The *Navigational Landmarks* are very specific lines drawn on the hoof relative to certain structures that are common to all equine hooves. There are eight such landmarks used in the Basic Guidelines.

48. The landmarks are derived from a 3 dimensional spatial grid, called the *Hoof Plexus*. This is an abstract network of horizontal and perpendicular lines, points, and planes, that facilitate the measuring of hoof size, proportion, and growth angles — the *Critical Measurements* — based on the theory of H°.

49. There are many *Critical Measurements* derived from the Hoof Plexus, but only two are used in the Basic Guidelines. These are very specific measurements for toe angle (H°) and toe length (H°TL) that are unique to natural hoof care based on the wild horse model.

50. There are two additional Critical Measurements of interest, B° and B°TL. These measurements are corollaries of H° and H°TL, arising from capsule deformity due to pathology. Technically, however, they are the providence of the Advanced Guidelines.

51. All hoof mapping begins with the Median Axis of the Volar Profile (MAVP).

[Note to student: from this point forward — pages 54 to 64 — is your introduction to gridding the hooves for the Navigational Landmarks and then determining values for H° and H°TL. This will be the primary focus of your Step 2 Clinic; thus, spending considerable time here studying these pages is highly recommended to prepare you for the hand's-on applications with your clinician. Practicing on the front hooves of your own horse/s is also recommended.]

52. The MAVP-MATW Joint ("MM-Joint") connects the volar and mediolateral profiles of the hoof in such a way as to set the stage for measuring H° and H°TL.

53. Technically, the MM-Joint joint occurs where the MATW is formed, namely at the juncture of the MAVP with the outer wall of the *s. medium* — or the *s. tectorium* if the latter is not worn or rasped away.

54. The MATW is drawn in alignment with the "grain" of the hoof — i.e., the horn tubules visible in the *s. medium*.

55. The bull's-eye (◉) is a single point on the face of the toe wall enabling us to find H°, H°TL, and B°TL.

56. The MPTW is defined as an imaginary plane — think of a pane of glass but without any physical mass ("matterless mass")! — that passes through the bull's-eye and the entire hoof at a right angle (90°) to the SP.

57. To measure H°, the hoof's support pillars must all be placed on SP.

58. B° and B°TL are two additional Critical Measurements that you should be aware of, as they are very likely to show up in most horses today due to the international epidemic of WHID.

59. B° and B°TL are pathological corruptions of H° and H°TL.

[Note to student: In addition to this quiz, take the Chapter 5 Quiz on pp. 71-72 in the Basic Guidelines; an answer key is provided at the back of the book.]

60. *Active* and *passive* wear are significant characteristics of the naturally shaped hoof. They represent the natural convolutions of the hoof wall's ground-bearing surface.

61. *Active wear* typically occurs in groups of 3 support pillars (medial toe wall and both heel-buttresses); these groups are also called support triads.

62. SP is used to define VP. However, this does not mean that VP is naturally balanced, only that it has been located. More information is needed to define or make a determination of hoof balance.

63. H°TL is the shortest possible length of the toe wall that can be trimmed without penetrating the HSP.

64. The objective of *nipper dragging* is to expose the HSP from toe to heel-buttresses.

65. *Frog notching* in conjunction with nipper dragging is an important and useful technique to confirm both the HSP and *heel length*.

66. Balancing the heels sets the stage for balancing the entire hoof.

67. After the heels are balanced, MLHA is determined (and, thus, the Hard Frog Plane), and the heel-buttresses are brought to their optimal length, the result is a balanced hoof relative to SP.

68. Mastery of the *Basic Guidelines* is crucial to understanding the *Advanced Guidelines*, and attempts to trim deformed hooves — the temptation of many beginners — without HTLA confirmed leads directly to invasive trimming.

69. If a horse is living in a stall, a walled paddock, or a grass pasture, the hooves given a natural trim will not be naturally balanced. Balanced? Artificially so, *possibly*. Naturally balanced? *Not at all.*

[Note to student: From page 88 to 90 lies the principal defense of horses going barefoot. The conventional argument for the "hoof mechanism" is that the horseshoe is needed to *protect and support* the hoof under the weight of the rider, if not the horse themself going barefoot. Because the wild horse model is still rejected or ignored by mainstream veterinary science, it is the burden of the NHC practitioner to counter this misguided science. The NHC model for the hoof mechanism points not only to the reality of the wild horse, but to an entirely different premise of weight-bearing by the horse's foot. This discussion began in your studies of *The Natural Horse*, so review the same material here again to confirm your ability to defend the wild horse model.]

70. It is logical that sequencing should assume a core role in trimming horses, even though trimming per se is not defined by sequencing, nor vice versa.

71. Efficiency during the natural trim means having the tools "homed" in the hoof stand — every tool has its own place on the stand and is kept there until used, and returned to its home once the task is completed.

72. Relative dominance, or "RD" as I call it, refers to the horse's natural instinct to establish his position in the specie's pecking order.

73. Sooner or later, most horses will "test" the trimmer by breaking sequence to see if they can control the situation, just as they would do in the wild.

74. My standard policy and recommendation is to not trim or have anything to do with abused horses. Our job is to trim, not rehabilitate traumatized animals.

75. Horses are incredibly perceptive and intelligent and know when you are playing them versus when you are sincere. They are also discriminating of competent and incompetent trimmers, but are likely to be more cooperative if they are rewarded for being patient!

76. To facilitate optimal understanding between our species, I use and teach two fundamental communication skills: "ear radar" and "pressuring the muscle ring."

77. The position and movement of the horse's ears reveals a lot about his feelings and behavior. This is called "ear radar."

78. Ear radar and pressure points on the muscle ring connect into the specie's responsiveness based on relative dominance. Learning to read the horse's radar and apply pressure with discretion and praise/rewards will elevate the trimmer higher in the social hierarchy, commanding respect and cooperation.

79. Horses are very perceptive and discriminating, and will readily exploit to a lower position of relative dominance those trimmers who are not in shape and are struggling to sequence. This can mean different things, all of them unpleasant.

80. Battles between horses and farriers are legend in the horse world, virtually all of it unnecessary when the principles of sequencing are understood, confirmed, and practiced. Barefooters are not exempt from such outcomes either.

81. The *support diagonals* are derived from the specie's natural gait complex (NGC) and, therefore, are readily assumed by the horse when commanded by the trimmer (or Handler) using RD.

82. The *5 Basic Positions* are an amalgamation of techniques I learned many years ago as a farrier, what I learned later from wild and domesticated horses, innovations that coincided with the development of new tools and equipment, and the requirements of the natural trim itself to do it correctly in keeping with the wild horse model.

83. "Deep and low" is used in all positions, wherein the trimmer can brace their elbows on their thighs for work, rest, and relieving the lower back of stress during trimming.

84. Because of the orderliness of sequencing, the horse readily participates knowing when and where the trimmer, handler, and tools/equipment are at in each of the

5 Basic Positions.

Final Notes to Student:

- From pages 107 to 143 (Chapter 9) I delineate each of the "10 distinct steps" of the natural trim. Logically, this information will remain largely an abstraction — words not rooted in practice — until your Step 2 clinic, later your Step 4 clinic, and finally, your Field Mentorships. Nevertheless, go diligently through the descriptions absorbing what you can. It is highly recommended that you study this chapter during your Step 2 clinic "off time" to draw lines between what you have read and then practiced under your clinician's guiding hand.

- Chapter 10 (pp. 144-159) concerns shoe pulling. Clinicians may or may not emphasize this in their clinics, and personally, I discourage student involvement with de-shoeing altogether. It is part of farriery, per se, not NHC. Instead, my advice is to make it your future client's responsibility to have their a farrier remove the shoes but, subsequently, not trim the hooves. But this is only my advice, and you should discuss the prospect of teaching shoe pulling with your clinician in advance of Step 2. If that is the case, then study Chapter before Step 2.

The Natural Trim
Principles and Practice

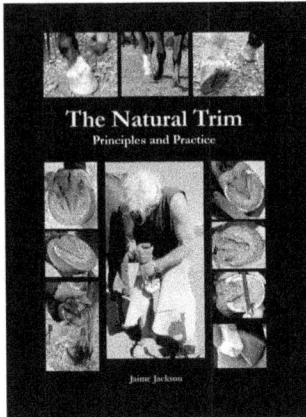

The Natural Trim: Principles and Practice (2019 edition) is the immediate ancestor of the Basic Guidelines (2019 edition), and fourth generation of the original *Horse Owners Guide to Natural Hoof Care* dating back to its earliest 1996 iteration (now out of print). Referred to as "TNT," *Principles and Practice* contains much information, including a history of NHC, that is not included in the *Basic Guidelines*. *TNT* also includes important information on Sequencing and a technical method for diagnosing Navicular Syndrome.

    TNT is divided into two parts. *Part I: Principles*, provides NHC history not included in *The Natural Horse*. Also included is prehistoric information about *Equus ferus ferus*, including DNA studies, and the animal's catastrophic demise in North America 8-10,000 years ago in the Late Pleistocene Epoch. Several chapters follow discussing natural wear patterns, structures of the hoof, and the Healing Angle ("Theory of H°"). A complete discussion of the NHC "Hoof Mechanism" is cast in an analysis of competing theories, concluding *Part I*.

    Part II opens with a discussion of *relative dominance* (RD) as a means to communicate with the horse based on wild horse behavior. Within the context of RD, also taken up are working with the horse's diagonals, giving praise, the value of treating correctly, the complementary roles of the Trimmer and Handler, and the 5 Basic Positions of Sequencing. From these discussions until the end of the book are brief instructions for trimming horses having no lameness issues to those suffering the most severe and debilitating imaginable. Trimming instructions in these chapters are to be ignored by students in the Basic Natural Trim Training Program. Most of this information is the providence of the *Advanced Guidelines*.

TNT: P&P Quiz

1. Until more recent centuries, the historical record shows that most horses have been ridden unshod since their domestication 8,000 or more years ago.

2. With the advent of the Industrial Revolution in the late 18th century, most European, and later American, horses were routinely shod.

3. By 1900, most horse owners had no memory of the pre-horseshoeing days, such had become the convention of horseshoeing.

4. The "jump" to NHC did not occur overnight, however. It began rather slowly, and, admittedly, cautiously, with certain of my professional shoeing clients who seemed open-minded to the possibilities.

5. Interest in NHC was never confined to the United States, indeed, from the outset, it arose simultaneously in Europe, the UK, countries of the Middle East, Australia, New Zealand, Mexico, Chile, and other places. More recently, interest has come from countries once held hostage behind the Iron Curtain of Soviet control.

6. NHC is still relatively new to the horse-using community compared to the 800 year farrier tradition.

7. Rejecting the value of "wildness" in the horse, in a sense, is foolish because it means rejecting the horse's biological roots.

8. Feral horses, like domesticated horses, genetically speaking, are all derived from the same wild animal, *Equus ferus ferus*. Meaning, they are still the same species.

9. The difference, then, between wild horses at the dawn of domestication upon the Eurasian steppes thousands of years ago and all horses today, is not in variant species, but in the wilderness and domesticated *experiences*.

10. Natural selection is the process by which those heritable traits (e.g., hair color serving as camouflage or sexual attraction) that make it more likely for an organism to survive and successfully reproduce become more common in a population over successive generations.

11. Scientists studying the genetic evolution of the horse believe that the modern horse, *Equus ferus caballus* evolved through natural selection over a stretch of 55 million years following the extinction of the last dinosaurs in the Cretaceous Period, arriving as we know them today (based on their DNA) approximately 1.4 to 1.7 million years ago, long before the dawn of humans.

12. By the time the Spanish arrived in the American southwest, the region more closely resembled the semi-arid Eurasian steppes where *Equus ferus ferus* had long ago survived, flourished, and became domesticated — at the same time members of his species perished in Late Pleistocene North America.

13. As it turns out, not all wild horse or "feral" herds are suitable as models for NHC and the natural trim as they do not inhabit the high desert type *biome* (ecosystem) of their specie's ancient adaptation.

14. Both the Duelmener and Dartmoor horses — typically suffering from laminitis — as with many other feral horse populations in the world, are simply poor study groups for NHC practitioners due to their non-adaptive habitats.

15. The world of NHC is built upon four inseparable and defining foundational pil-

lars: *natural boarding, a reasonably natural diet, natural horsemanship, and the natural trim.*

16. Regarding the matter of natural horsemanship . . . there is no good and reliable system of horsemanship based on our wild horse model.

[Note to student: From page 41 to page 48 is one of the more detailed descriptions of how the Lompoc, California Paddock Paradise was put together in 2010. So this is worth reading closely. Although it evolved over the next eight years this is the only such detailed description to date.]

17. Horse feeds should be free of sweeteners such as molasses, cane or beet sugar, sugar beet pulp, and high fructose corn syrup, as all of these have been implicated in laminitis.

18. Avoid all grass pasture turnouts, except the natural Great Basin types foraged by wild, free-roaming horses, as these also are implicated in laminitis.

19. There is considerable anecdotal evidence that chemical parasiticides and vaccinations may also be triggers for laminitis in horses.

20. The Mongols of East-Central Asia use horses for their transportation, as they have for thousands of years. Their horses are neither trimmed nor shod, and their hooves are exemplary by NHC standards.

[Note to student: Chapters 3, 4, and 5 are sufficiently covered, and even updated here and there, in your other readings as to require not much more than a close reading. Having said this, one part of Chapter 5 is worth quizzing you on here as it will surface in your Final Written Exam.]

21. The "Four Guiding Principles of the Natural Trim" are based entirely on the wild horse model. Therefore, they connect us directly to the laws of nature and the powerful forces of adaptation that created the horse's foot through the evolutionary descent of *Equus ferus caballus* through natural selection.

22. Guiding Principle #1, "Leave that which naturally should be there," refers to the protection and preservation by the trimmer of the integrity of the basic anatomical parts of the hoof, such as the frog, bars, sole, and hoof wall.

23. Guiding Principle #2, "Remove only that which is naturally worn away in the wild," means that when the hoof (i.e., epidermis or capsule) is reduced by the trimmer, only that which would be worn away in the horse's wild state is taken.

24. Guiding Principle #3, "Allow to grow that which should be there naturally but isn't due to human meddling," instructs the trimmer to use restraint when faced with hooves that have been over trimmed in some part.

25. Guiding Principle #4, "Ignore all pathology," warns the trimmer not to focus on pathology (if present) or violations of the three previous principles, but, instead, to look intuitively to 4th-dimensional changes (healing changes over time — "respect the healing powers of nature") and to faithfully adhere to NHC principles and practices.

26. The natural trim (governed by the *Four Guiding Principles*) triggers a cascade of integrated biodynamic (i.e., living) forces that produce and reinforce naturally shaped hooves. This melding of forces is sometimes described as a reinforcing "cycle of form and function."

Final note to student:

- Chapter 6 visits the *Healing Angle* (H°) and related critical measurements. Reading this entire chapter closely can't but help reinforce and clarify earlier discussions in *The Natural Horse* and the *Basic Guidelines*. Some of the discussions cross over into deformed hooves — this is material not included in this training program, but feel free to go through it with the understanding that it lays outside the scope of what you will be held accountable for.

- Chapter 7 revisits the *Hoof Mechanism*. Of interest is the presentation of conflicting viewpoints on the Mechanism. Students should take from this reading what the consequences are of adopting one over another, particularly as its theories are applied to the hoof.

- The *Introduction to Part II* of *Principles and Practice* (pages 159 to 175) concludes the required reading in this text. The section on *RD* and *support diagonals* is, to my way of thinking, very important. Especially if you don't want to get hurt working with horses, particularly with horses you don't know or know anything about, and, at that, being under such horses in close contact.

- Chapter 15 is something you can look over briefly. This is the NHC *specialized dissection* you will be taught and doing in your Step 2 Clinic.

- Chapter 16 is more on de-shoeing, but your previous reading assignment in the *Basic Guidelines* provides the same information. Review here at your discretion.

- The *Glossary* and *Index of NHC Terms* is there to help you quickly locate and review words and definitions in the text that you should know.

the Hoof Balancer
A Unique Tool For
Balancing Equine Hooves

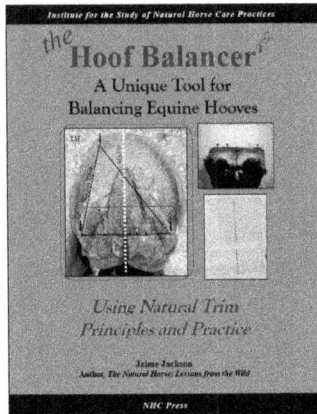

the Hoof Balancer: A Unique Tool For Balancing Equine Hooves (2017 edition) is an instructional book for the Hoof Balancer tool. This tool provides us with a quick, easy, accurate, and efficient way to balance the hoof when conducting the natural trim. It is a great learning tool for students when deployed on both cadaver and live hooves, but is also recommended for use by all hoof care practitioners in the field, particularly when confronted with extreme capsule deformity.

The earliest version of the Balancer tool evolved out of the Hoof Meter Reader in the 1980s. The HMR requires a support plane to measure H° and H°TL, but locating active and passive wear would be more easily evaluated if the SP were "mobile," as opposed to stationary ground. The latter not always being available, the first Balancer tool was the answer, providing not only an SP but one that enabled the trimmer to see through it to the volar profile beneath at the same time. This first version had no "window" nor did it have the medial axis groove.

As my understanding of the wild horse hoof progressed, the addition of the center groove enabled me to pin point active wear relative to the Medial Axis of the Volar Profile (MAVP). Mediolateral hoof balance across the heels then began gradually to reveal itself as I sought out useful Navigational Landmarks. It wasn't long before I began to sense and then "see" in my mind's eye the existence of the three-dimensional Hoof Plexus. Within this plexus came the solution I was looking for. The window was added to help me accurately sight the hoof in an entirely new way. I introduced the first Balancers in my clinics in 2000.

Sighting the hoof mediolaterally across the back of the hoof is typically a great challenge for students and even professionals. This stems directly from not balancing the heels relative to the Median Plane of the Volar Profile (MPVP) — the theoretical second plane of the Hoof Plexus and the pathway to the *Mediolateral Heel Axis* (MLHA). The untrained eye will naturally gravitate to the medial heel and sight the hoof from there across to the medial heel, or vice versa. Here the trouble begins, as both active and passive wear forward of the heels "argue" with the eye for preeminence in the two-dimensional VP. And who is to say which is correct?* Much teetering of the hoof from side to side to find one's way invariably leads to the lateral heel appearing too long. But this is the burden of the barefoot practitioner to solve alone, as the farrier dispenses of any such conflict instantaneously by simply flattening the entire VP to set the shoe. *the Hoof Balancer* book and Balancer tool are my interventions to help elucidate natural order from disorder in the eye of the NHC student.

*Common "solutions" are to align the VP or MLHA at 90° to the pastern, to make the heels the same length, to make one heel longer than the other, to make the horse "stand straight," to flatten the entire VP, to shoe the hoof with heel wedges, and so forth. Solutions are often what are "fashionable" or arbitrary rather than rooted in nature. Logically, "corrective" trimming and shoeing can trace their origins to the variant and arbitrary fashions of the times.

the Hoof Balancer Quiz

1. The meaning of "balanced hooves" in the hoof care world is rife with unsubstantiated opinions and methods that compromise the natural integrity of the hoof and the ability of the horse to move naturally.

2. The *Hoof Balancer Tool* (functioning as SP) is used for two purposes: to determine the location of *active* and *passive wear* in the hoof's Volar Plane, which serve to define natural *hoof balance*; and in sighting and marking the *Mediolateral Heel Axis* (MLHA), which defines *heel balance* — an inseparable and consummating dimension of natural hoof balance.

3. The *Hoof Balancer* can be used at any time during the course of the natural trim.

4. The *Hoof Balancer* will require a working knowledge of three Navigational Landmarks derived from the Hoof Plexus: the *MAVP, MPVP* and *MLHA*.

5. The groove of the *Hoof Balancer* is aligned with the MAVP sighted or drawn on the hoof.

6. To find MLHA, the Balancer is held at the back of the hoof at an angle and then aligned with the same reference points that also define the MAVP: *cleft of the heel bulbs, central cleft (sulcus) of the frog,* and *point of frog.*

7. The *Mediolateral Heel Axis* (MLHA) is a single cut-line drawn across the back of both heels and the frog; it lies at a right angle (90°) to the MPVP.

8. By definition of the *Hoof Plexus*, the MLHA is perpendicular (90°) to the SP; therefore, it is also parallel with the ground.

9. The wild horse model dictates that the natural trim guidelines are *not* concerned with the relative locations of the heels toward or away from the MAVP. Nor are they concerned with their relative locations toward or away from the toe pillar. Finally, they are not concerned with the actual measurable lengths of the heels from the coronary band to the SP. Instead, the guidelines are concerned only with heel length — whatever each might be — relative to the MLHA.

10. Without the *Hoof Plexus*, there would be no logical way to deduce natural heel balance.

11. The upper or lower edge of the *Hoof Balancer's* window is set level with the frog after it has been trimmed to its natural size, or to where its natural length has been determined by "frog notching."

12. A black ink Sharpie is used to mark the MLHA on the back of each heel; these are the cut-lines for lowering and balancing the heels.

13. *Active and passive wear* can be located by passing a piece of paper or thin object between the hoof wall and the *Hoof Balancer.*

14. The frog should be level with or just passive to the *Hoof Balancer.*

15. Placement and positioning of the *Hoof Balancer* against the back of the hoof is critical if the MLHA is to be marked correctly.

16. Allowing one's focus to shift above or below the Balancer's upper or lower window edge will result in a parallax shift of the MLHA.

17. Aligning the *Hoof Balancer's* grooved line to the MPVP, and then aligning one's focus on either window edge, will minimize or preclude any parallax corruption of the MLHA.

Paddock Paradise
A Guide to
Natural Horse Boarding

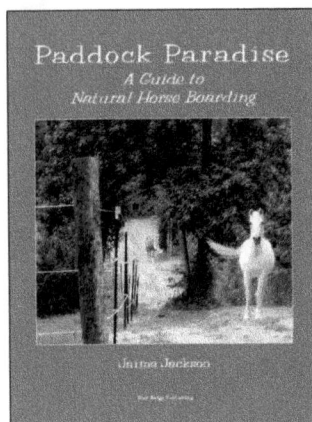

Paddock Paradise: A guide to Natural Horse Boarding (2018 edition) is the NHC foundational work for natural horse boarding. While I wrote this book over several years (late 2004 until I first published it in late 2005), I began talking about its principles much earlier — publicly dating back into the 1990s. sans its peculiar sobriquet. But the vision for it came earlier still, in fact, in wild horse country.

Following one of my sojourns into the back country, I went to visit one of the HMA field managers in his office at the BLM's headquarters for the wild horse and burro program (administered in accordance with the 1970 legislation) in Carson City. I told him I had began to see the home ranges as a complex labyrinth of trails, or paths, that each wild horse family band traveled upon with a certain regularity. In fact, with such regularity you could "hold them to a clock." He thought about it and agreed. On a piece of paper, I drew a circle representing a water hole. From the hole I drew what looked like a haphazard conglomeration of "loops" that trailed to and from the water hole. I handled him the pen, and he drew a second water hole, and we connected the water holes together taking turns with the pen. I added, "It's all organized by the horses. It's how they travel and live. They live in loops." He hadn't really thought of it that way. His job, like other managers, was to monitor their numbers and get crews ready to remove them from the wild.

But for me, upon returning home to my clients, the clash between organized movements of horses versus horses living at standstill in stalls, corrals, and lush pastures, was practically unbearable. But to suggest such a thing as a simple "possibility" to my clients was to invite confusion and even anger or laughter. Horses moving freely on their own in domestication was simply out of the question. But resistance was something I was already accustomed to. A few years earlier in 1982 I had suggested that I do a "wild horse trim" to a client's horse. The idea of putting something "wild" on their horse was too much. The response was a cross between a scream and total outrage. I dropped it. The wild horse trim eventually evolved into "the natural trim." *Natural* seemed okay with people. No mention of or connection to wild horses.

Paddock Paradise (not yet phrased) continued to elude me. Conceptually it was much more difficult to put together, other than "lives living in loops." Eventually, the breakthrough came through. But it was the wild horse that came to my rescue, and at that, wild horses captive in the BLM corrals. Chapter 2 explains what happened. Yet I held that revelation silently in abeyance for nearly 25 years before daring to "come out of the closet" with it and write the book. That was 15 years ago. And the concept has since grown its own wings, like Pegasus, forming its own constellation in a galaxy of "lessons from the wild" people are still discovering and making happen.

Paddock Paradise Quiz

1. The horse naturally must be free to move constantly, and everything depends on it for his mental and physical well-being and soundness.

2. I discovered that the very lifestyle of the wild horse, driven by natural behavior, lay at the bottom of optimum hoof form and health.

3. Paddock Paradise aims to open the door to the missing freedom and lifestyle of the domesticated horse's natural world by situating and propelling the animal forward in an unprecedented environmental configuration that, holistically speaking, both stimulates and facilitates natural movement.

4. Wild horse society is comprised of family groups, never isolated individuals.

5. To the uninitiated human eye, one would readily conclude that band movements are random, and that the actual home range is without "boundaries" in the mind of the horse. But neither is the case at all, and, thus well-defined space and structured movement through it comprise yet another invaluable "lesson from the wild."

6. At the heart of the home range are one or more water holes. All band movements center around these. The tracks leading away from the water holes, sooner or later turn back to them, depending on temperature and thirst.

7. BLM managers in the early days of government gathers learned quickly that wild horse families "on track" do not like to leave their home ranges.

8. The better our picture of the wild horse's natural behaviors, the better able we will be to provide similar opportunities within Paddock Paradise.

9. Wild horses at the water hole, particularly during warm months, will often roll in the dirt, if not in the water, in order to muddy-up their coats. This is "rolling behavior" and it constitutes an important lesson from the wild."

10. Grazing behavior in the wild is a slow, mouth-to-the-ground, eat-n-go affair along and near their paths.

11. Much of the wild horse diet appears to be range grasses and grass-like plants, and probably a wide variety of high desert type legumes.

12. Some researchers have reported that wild horses spend roughly half their daily lives eating.

13. In wild horse country, there are favorite sleeping areas away from perceived threats, both in open and not-so-open country where predator movement is more readily detected.

14. In the same way that thirst regulates the degree of track movement away from the water hole, so does the availability of forage and other vital nutrients, stallion rivalry, and pressure from predators, impact the speed of movement on a given track.

15. Another "lesson from the wild" is that we should make every effort to "dress up" Paddock Paradise in the simple name of natural beauty.

16. Wild horses will use their hooves to dig up vital mineral (calcium) deposits and then grind them up with their teeth . . . a way of managing their own teeth while meeting important nutritional needs. In PP, it may aid or substitute the veterinary practice of rasping the dental arcades.

17. Numerous theories are being presented as to what is normal tooth structure, what abnormalities are correctable, and how much correction should be done. To date, no controlled documented studies have been presented to show the benefits of aggressive rasping of the dental arcades, especially to the table surfaces of equine teeth.

18. Equine and bovine, and occasional mule deer and antelope, are complementary feeders and do not compete aggressively for available forage. Each "stays to its own" and go there own way.

19. There is a subtle temptation to disperse — that is, to fan out across the plain where others can't compete for every mouthful of grass. But the "herding" instinct for self-preservation — again, the ubiquitous threat of the stealthful cougar — is too powerful to tolerate dispersion. Nor would alpha stallions allow it.

20. "Mutual grooming" has an important ritualistic place in bonding between horses as well a deterrent to aberrant behavior stemming from isolation.

21. It may be that in Paddock Paradise, if configured closely after our wild model, horse worming may not be necessary or even desirable.

22. Immense beds of pulverized, sharp-edged, igneous rock from these lava flows carpet large areas of wild horse country. Yet, our horses move over them effortlessly and without any apparent hypersensitivity or deleterious effect upon their feet.

23. Wild mares may form a "mares' circle" to rest and ignore the commotion of battling stallions, but also a defense formation used to protect the young when predators threaten the herd.

24. At the water hole, many bands converge, as though on notice to do so at the same time. As many as 100 horses may be present, each band taking turns in order of relative dominance.

25. The water hole interaction is an important time in the sexual selection of wild horse society. Young females leave or are driven off by their fathers to find their mates. Some older stallions are unseated by a younger generation, and older mares may elect to leave with a deposed senior. Or a more aggressive or astute male will simply de-throne an aging alpha male. A myriad of possibilities.

26. Some researchers have cited as many as 200 different legumes comprising about 10% of the bulk diet. Consistent with my own field observations is the Hansen, et al. finding that the wild horse diet is comprised mainly of grasses and sedges, although altitude and regional biomes will cause shifts in eating behavior based on availability of specific forage. What this means is that the wild horse diet is far more adaptable and complex than most of us can begin to imagine.

27. As time went by, I began to speculate that natural wear may only arise from natural behavior, such as we see in the wild — behavior that we seldom see among domesticated horses. And to a lesser extent, from the effects of environment.

28. The "lessons from the wild" described in Chapter 1 provide us with the essential guidelines for constructing Paddock Paradise.

29. First, you don't need a large property for Paddock Paradise. You don't need land the size of a typical home range. In fact, the larger your property is, proportionally the less of it you will need to use! Again, it's how we use the land, not how much we own.

30. Paddock Paradise also ignores the shape of your property, which can be any shape

(or size). In fact, the final design of your Paddock Paradise will be up to you and you can adapt it to all or part of your property.

31. In Paddock Paradise we are going to literally confine him to his "track" (with a few diversions spaced here and there), in effect preventing him from dispersing and doing nothing. Activities along the way will provide the necessary stimuli to motivate him to move along forward on track.

32. It was my observation in wild horse country that movement based on ordinary behavior constituted about 95 percent of their locomotive energy expended; extraordinary behavior only 5 percent, or less.

33. Paddock Paradise is the horse's home, or more precisely, his home range. I believe we should respect it as such, and, for the most part, stay out of it.

34. My research of the wild horse diet suggests that horses will benefit from being fed a mix of grass-type hays, unsweetened oats in small quantities, mineral and salt licks, and water. Until we learn more about the horse's natural diet, I would caution horse owners from feeding much of anything else, particularly horses suffering or recovering from laminitis.

35. What we want to do is spread the feed, particularly the hay, around the track at regulated intervals. The idea is to space the hay so that the horses will keep moving. If we place too much in one spot, or in only one location, we will encourage "camping." Camping is okay, but it shouldn't be feeding behavior based.

36. There seem to be two distinct patterns of rolling behavior in wild horse country. One is a "mud" bath and occurs in relation to the water hole, the other occurs elsewhere on track and is more of a "dusting" experience.

37. I believe the terrain through which the track passes should be as interesting and diverse as we can make it. If sections of your land are convoluted, if it has a stream or a pond, is wooded, rocky, whatever, direct the track into those areas. We want the horse to work his body and his feet. Flat land is okay too, but . . ?"

Laminitis
An Equine Plague Of
Unconscionable Proportions

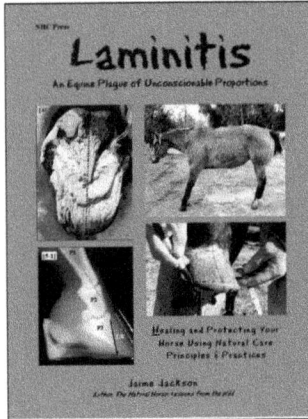

Laminitis: An Equine Plague Of Unconscionable Proportions (2016 edition) is a second generation upgrade of an earlier related work, *Founder: Prevention and Cute the Natural Way* (2001, Star Ridge Publishing). *Founder*, nineteen years later, is still popular with many horse owners, but like everything else based on the wild horse model, NHC science has not stood still but advanced. The principal change concerns the pathogenesis of laminitis: once thought to be a disease of the foot, now understood to be a symptom of WHID — Whole Horse (or Whole Body) Inflammatory Disease.

To understand laminitis, NHC science holds that we must look away from the hoof and to the whole body of the horse to understand what's actually going on. And, technically speaking, that's not enough. Because WHID's origin lies in what we put into the horse. This can be feeds, pasture turnout, vaccinations, medications, parasiticides, in short, anything we put into the horse that their body cannot metabolize. While *Founder* also interpreted laminitis as a consequence of WHID — if not in name, then in terms of causality — *Laminitis: A Plague* redefines it as one of many symptoms of WHID.

Because WHID originates itself pathologically in the horse's body as an infestation of specific bacteria, bacteria that are infecting horses worldwide, I decided to cast it further as a "plague." One introduced and spread by humans unwittingly through feeding and veterinary practices.

Laminitis—A Plague Quiz

1. Laminitis is, in fact, an enormous profiteering racket that feeds the voracious appetite of what can only be called a "laminitis industry."

2. Laminitis is actually an inflammatory disease of the whole horse with symptoms that erupt in many parts of the horse's body, including the feet.

3. Laminitis is a symptom of what I understand to be a Whole Horse Inflammatory Disease (WHID).

4. Technically, laminitis is the pathological separation of the hoof from the horse, one of many symptoms of WHID.

5. The conventional definition of laminitis used most often by veterinarians, farriers and barefoot trimmers, and horse owners who've had to deal with it, is *inflammation of the (dermal) lamina*, hence the term *laminitis*.

6. *Lamina* refers to the network of dermal and epidermal leaf-like structures that interlock together to form a complex bridge of connective tissue between the inner hoof wall and the outer face of the lowermost bone of the horse's foot, called the coffin bone — known variously as the pedal bone, distal phalanx, and P3.

7. The body of a dermal leaf is comprised of fibrous connective tissue, and is both vascular (contains blood) and innervated (contains nerves).

8. *The* epidermal leaves, in contrast to the dermal leaves, are also fibrous, but are neither enervated nor vascular.

9. The dermal and epidermal leaves are connect together to form the Lamellar Attachment Mechanism, or "LAM."

10. Not visible to the naked eye, is another component of each dermal leaf called the *basal* or *basement membrane*. This is a thin membranous layer of connective tissue that covers the underlying vascular tissue of the dermal leaf.

11. Epithelial cells continuously proliferate from the basement membrane to form the *secondary epidermal leaves (lamina)*, or SEL. As each SEL is produced, it adheres to the "host" PEL through cellular migration and integration.

12. Through the actions of specialized enzymes operative in the environment (called proteolysis), the cellular bonds between the PELs and SELs are cleaved and replaced by new generations of proliferating epithelial cells. In this way, the hoof wall (including the attached PELs) is detached and able to grow down past the stationary SELs, basement membrane and the underlying connective tissue of the dermal leaves, to which P3 is attached.

13. Laminitis is set off in the lower intestine by substances consumed (sweet feeds, medications, supplements, etc.) or injected medications such as antibiotics, sedatives, pain killers, steroids, vaccinations, etc.) that favor the proliferation of harmful hind gut bacteria.

14. Hind gut bacterial contamination impact enzymes naturally present in the LAM responsible for breaking down the epithelial cells so that the hoof can naturally descend past P3. These enzymes now proliferate pathologically, destroying the cellular bonds that are responsible for securing the wall to P3 and faster than normal mechanisms involved can repair them.

15. If proteolysis is not halted by appropriate changes in the horse's diet, the LAM

will continue to degrade and eventually become a tangled mass of disorganized growth.

16. Degradation of the LAM is accompanied by inflammatory symptoms within the foot, particularly during acute attacks; these may include severe pain, elevated temperatures, and a palpable pounding pulse above the coronary band.

17. Ignoring causality and nature's healing pathways, conventional care has resulted in treatment strategies that are typically and unnecessarily mechanical, invasive, ineffective, and worse, damaging not only to the foot, but to the horse's overall well-being.

18. Treating laminitis as though it originates or is limited to the foot is an invitation to disaster.

19. "Cresty necks," obesity, psychological distress, hives, itchy skin, appearing to be arthritic, and other types of lameness are all symptomatic of laminitic horses, but also of WHID.

20. Stated simply, laminitis *triggers* are any substances, natural or artificial, that distress the horse's metabolic processes resulting in laminitis.

21. Sugars in all forms are triggers, yet many horse feeds include significant amounts of molasses, sugar beet pulp, and/or cane sugar.

22. Artificial triggers are those biological, chemical, and agricultural products manufactured by the laminitis industry.

23. In short, while there are many possible laminitis triggers, not all horses may react the same to them. *At least in the short term.*

24. Treating and presenting laminitis works like this: *known* triggers are removed entirely (or mostly so) from the horse's lifestyle, and the horse is then brought into the broad, holistic fold of NHC based on the wild horse model.

25. Laminitis pathophysiology occurs in three stages of progressive development: *sub-clinical (absence of pain)* → *clinical (observable pain)* → *chronic (sub-clinical + clinical)*.

26. The *sub-clinical stage* of laminitis is characterized by no observable pain.

27. The *clinical stage* of laminitis is characterized by observable pain, obstruction of the natural gaits, and other overt changes in the horse's body, demeanor and metabolic processes.

28. Symptoms of the *chronic stage of* laminitis tend to be off and on, and may include any of the previous symptoms (sub-clinical and clinical) plus a range of possible hoof deformities, aberrant upper body hair growth, dysfunctional internal organs, inability to move naturally, and neurotic psychological distress.

29. Founder, technically, is a consequence of laminitis. The term is often used synonymously with laminitis, but there is a difference. Specifically, founder means that the lowermost bone of the horse's foot has separated from the hoof wall due to a catastrophic failure of the LAM.

[Study note to student: From Chapter 6 until the end of the book, the primary focus is on rehabilitative efforts to help the laminitic horse. While these are important chapters to study at this point in your training, they are arguably best understood in the context of your field training (i.e., the Field Mentorships), when you will un-doubted begin to run into laminitic horses suffering minor deformity. Remember, the thrust of your education focuses on the Basic Guidelines of the natural trim — not the Advanced Guidelines. The Basic natural trim needs to be mastered before venturing into laminitis pathology. So, in these chapters, approach them from the standpoint of humane management protocols (4 Pillars of NHC) based on the wild horse model, rather than what you think you can glean from them to trim laminitic horses. For this reason, there are no trimming instructions in this book.]

Online Study Assignments

- In addition to the required book reading assignments, there are additional assignments online. Go to the drop down menu, "NHC Published Articles/Bulletins" on the ISNHCP website. Under "English" and "Advocacy Bulletins," you will find lists of articles and bulletins to read. Two are of particular importance in the English article selection: "Spirit Of the Natural Horses" (by Jaime Jackson) and "The Wild Horse Foot" (by Dr. Ric Redden). Read all the advocacy Bulletins, in particular "Wild Horse Preservation Zones." (by Jaime Jackson).

- The ISNHCP has created a password protected website where you will be able to view and/or download additional reading assignments and videos. You will receive access information by email from the ISNHCP.

Appendix

Physical Conditioning Exercises For NHC Practitioners

by Jaime Jackson

Trimming horses requires that our students be in top physical and mental condition. This is necessary to prevent harm to yourself and the horse. So important is this facet of trimming that the ISNHCP requires students be in top shape if they are to proceed with training. The ISNHCP will not advance students past their Step 3 Sequencing Clinic if there performance is poor and it is clear that the exercises in this training manual have been ignored. Specific exercises are provided here as they will prepare your body for sequencing. Students who are insufficiently conditioned to sequence, will be required to undertaking additional physical training until evidence of strength and capability is confirmed by your sequencing clinician *and* video submission to the ISNHCP. Students with medically diagnosed physical or mental disabilities should report this information to the ISNHCP before training commences. *Note that this caveat is included in the ISNHCP training application form.*

Because horses are by nature "animals of prey," they possess strong fear and flight instincts if subjected to strange, erratic or threatening behavior from their human handlers, spectators (including the owner), and anything in the environment that gives them concern. For this reason, the ISNHCP reserves the right to dismiss any student from the training program who arrives under the influence of behavior modifying drugs, including narcotics, alcohol, and cannabis products. Likewise, students exhibiting violent behavior towards the horse, towards students or towards instructors may also be expelled from the training program. Students with a medical history of drug addiction problems or anger management issues should report this to the ISNHCP prior to training. *The ISNHCP reserves the right to require legal drug testing or psychological evaluation of any student.*

Recommended exercises

Everyone has their personal ideas about exercising and being fit. My idea is to throw this notion of "I know how to exercise and be fit" right out the window when it comes to what we do under horses. The great body builder Arnold Alois Schwarzenegger once wrote that his wife asked him to hold their newborn baby in his arms, but that he couldn't hold the baby without tiring in only a fraction of the time of his wife. His message was that muscles have to be prepared for the type of work they are going to perform. Not to pick on Arnold, but he wouldn't last half the time he spent holding his baby when under a horse. Our work requires a specialized development of our muscles and corresponding stamina. Everything discussed in the following pages is what I have been doing for most of my adult life under horses, and going back further, in the Army, and before that as a competitive gymnast on the "still rings."

We have several specific objectives in our NHC Exercise Program:

- Learn how to breathe for power moves.
- Develop your muscle mass and protect your joints.
- Adapt exercises for the 5 Basic Positions used in our work.
- Use the principle of "progressive development" — gradually build yourself up.

Exercising for Strength — 30 Minute Workout

Stretching

This is such an individualized thing to do, so everyone will have to figure this one out for themselves. I personally do mine standing up, bending this way and that depending on how I feel. I don't spend much time doing it either, probably less than 2 minutes, as my exercises really do 99% of it for me.

Push-ups

This is truly the great muscle building exercise that covers the entire body. Some very impressive athletes do nothing but push-ups for their exercises. World records are astonishing, in the tens of thousands non-stop! Some record holders do them on the backs of their hands! Others using just one arm. Some just one finger! The most knuckle push-ups in one hour by a woman is 1,206 by Eva Clarke (Australia) on 31 January 2014! Whoa! We won't go to such extremes, and I do hope these competitors aren't using steroids? I think a good number to shoot for is 100 push-ups in five sets of 20, spread out between the other exercises. You'll find that the sets get easier as time goes by as muscle mass develops with your breathing. It's amazing what the human body can do, when we try.

You will probably feel "muscle burn" as you fatigue. This is due to glucose breakdown by the body resulting in lactic acidosis (the chemistry is complex and even controversial[1]). If this occurs, simply stop, walk around or stretch a moment, rest, and then resume. It's perfectly natural and nature is just warning you to rest a few moments before continuing; when the burn subsides, continue. It happened

[1] $C_6H_{12}O_6 \rightarrow 2\ CH_3COCO^-_2 + 2\ H^+$

to me all the time as a gymnast and happens to me everyday that I exercise as I reach my self-imposed limits. No big deal! Also, as with any compression exercise, breathe in as you let yourself down, and blow out as you push upwards; whatever, just get enough oxygen to continue. If you are gasping for air, you're doing too much. Back off.

Shoot for one push-up per second.

If you can't do a single push-up with your body levered straight from head to toe, do them on your knees. If you can only do one or two, that's where you start. Over time, possibly many months, you will eventually graduate to knees off the ground. Actually knees on the ground is a harder to do a push-up than straight body because it lacks the "spring" afforded by your feet, calves, and even the interplay between your back and stomach muscles.

Obviously, you can't do a hundred at the onset (i.e., 5 sets of 20), so your goal will be whatever you are capable of doing over your 30 minute regime. I

Iron Cross, Jackson.

do 50 at the rate of one per second, breathing in and out with each push up — the world record is 134/minute done on the back of the hands!

So, do your push-ups in sets of whatever you are able to achieve at first, on your knees if you lack the arm strength needed to start. If you simply can't do push-ups but on your knees, that's okay, do them like that because it's still very effective. But work your way to a full body press, because it's easier! According to a study published in the Journal of Strength and Conditioning Research, the test subjects supported with their hands, on average, 69.16% of their body mass in the up position, and 75.04% in the down position during the traditional push-ups. In modified push-ups, where knees are used as the pivot point, subjects supported 53.56% and 61.80% of their body mass in up and down positions, respectively.[1] Nature will let you know eventually if you can do them levered (hands only). If

[1]Suprak, David N; Dawes, Jay; Stephenson, Mark D (February 2011). "The Effect of Position on the Percentage of Body Mass Supported During Traditional and Modified Push-up Variants". Journal of Strength and Conditioning Research. 25 (2): 497–503. doi:10.1519/JSC.0b013e3181bde2cf.

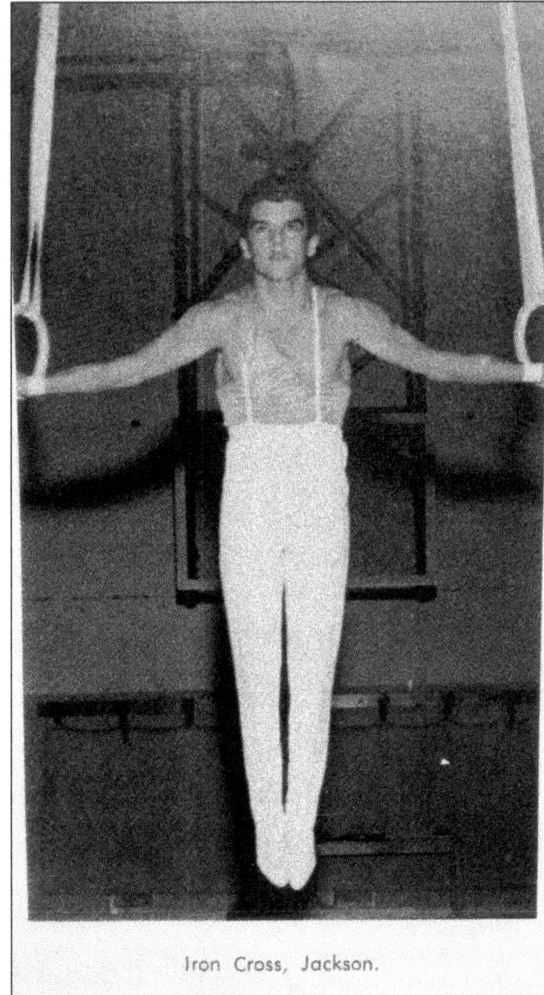

There are many variations of the push-up, one of the great "compression" based exercises for muscle development. Find your way to one or more of them. At age 73, I do 200 as part of my 30 minutes exercise regimen (and another 200 as part of my walking routine), but am conditioned to do 1,000 in about 4 to 5 hours. Here I am at 17 doing a push-up into a "planche" with my legs off the ground on my way to a handstand — which I also did on the rings! If you're new to the push-up, they're tough at first, but incredibly easier later if you follow the principle of *progressive development* — you can do it!

ISNHCP clinician takes the right hind hoof in the "deep n low" squat position. Not only a great exercise for developing strong legs and buttocks, as you can see, it has the potential for many applications in life that relieves the lower back of unnecessary stress and strain. Key to my ability to do this work in my 70s!

100 proves to be beyond your reach (five sets of 20 = 100), then pick a lower number and set that as a goal. The old saying, "Anything is better than nothing," applies here to get started. The important thing to understand is that it gets easier and easier — if you exercise regularly. Just like trimming horses gets easier and easier when you practice using the principle of progressive development.

Squats

Squats are another key exercise. I do 50 of these. My "rule" is to always have my feet in view during the squat and to keep my thighs higher than my knees — "above a parallel" crossing through my knee joints (photo *above*). Also, keep your heels at shoulder width — which we will integrate with Sequencing during your clinics and mentorships. Some experts claim that "high squats" (instead of low — below the parallel) put the lumber spine and knees at risk of injury over the long term. Well, at 60 years of doing them this way, I concur with other trainers who believe that high squats are one of the safest and best exercises for developing hip and leg muscles and strength. Likely, the problems occurred because of adding heavy (barbell) weights to the exercise and overloading the body. But since we don't do that, and there's no need to, our squats are perfectly safe.

I conclude my squat set by holding the final one for 60 seconds (or until lactosis forces me up!). I do this by bracing both of my forearms near the elbows on

my thighs just above the knees; I usually alternate by substituting one or both hands. I call this the "deep and low" position during trimming, and I use the heck out of it whenever I can — which is most of the time! Students are learning this in the above photo. Once your body is conditioned through all of these exercises, you'll be able to go deep/low to take breaks while under the horse! During such breaks in the deep/low, you're resting on your elbows with your stomach muscles relaxed and "hanging freely" until your body says otherwise when working or rising up when done.

The squat also prepares us to lift our tools/equipment with our powerful hip and leg muscles, rather than bending over at the waist to lift which is a sure way to injure your lower back (sciatica). So, squats are a very important part of your training because we use it on every hoof. And the good news is that by going deep/low in the squat, we are afforded rest time under the horse without having to leave the horse to take a break and recover. Moreover, a good deal of our trimming can be done efficiently and safely in the deep/low position. Learning to relax under the horse also sends a message to the horse to relax and that all is in good order. Notice in the photo several pages back that I'm slightly smiling during the "Iron Cross" on the still rings. Same thing, I'm actually pretty relaxed — and I was required by the rules to hold it for 4 to 5 seconds. During some routines, I would transform the cross into variations and sustain the position for 8 to 12 seconds more. Again, I couldn't do that at the beginning, but with progressive development I could.

Sit-ups

Like push-ups and squats, there's many ways to do sit-ups. I use nine variations I created totaling 150 — at one time I did 400 but was far more than I needed. The objective here is to tighten and release the stomach muscles, I do them laying flat on my back (*above*). I complete the sit-up exercises by balancing myself on my hips like the late famous exercise aficionado Jack LaLanne and his wife Elaine are demonstrating on the facing page. LaLanne and his wife lived in Moro Bay, just north of my home in Lompoc, before he passed away at age 96 in 2011. (Interesting family note: my Uncle George, who never exercised (but ate healthfully), passed away just a couple of years ago at age 101!). La-Lanne did amazing feats of strength, including 1,033 push-ups in 23 minutes at age 42 on TV in 1956! In 1984, at age 70 — handcuffed, shackled, and fighting strong winds and currents — he towed 70 rowboats, one with several persons aboard, one mile across the Long Beach Harbor in Southern California! Holy smokes! Not surprising, LaLanne was an inspiration to a young Arnold Schwarzenegger just arrived in the U.S. from Austria. Both worked out at famous "Muscle Beach" in Venice, CA. I was there a few times myself as they had still rings set up.

> "Dying is easy. Living is a pain in the butt. It's like an athletic event. You've got to train for it. You've got to eat right, you've got to exercise, your health account, your bank account, they're the same thing. The more you put in, the more you can take out. Exercise is king and nutrition is queen: together, you have a kingdom."
>
> Jack LaLanne

Hand grippers

I use these hand instruments primarily to big hand strength for nipper work. Some have adjustable spring tensioners, though I just use the $5 Wal-Mart gripper which works fine (*facing page*). Make sure the tension spring is something you can readily squeeze or you'll be complaining of *carpal tunnel syndrome* before long. I do fifty reps alternating squeezes between my left and right hands, then both hands simultaneously — all the while doing squats and taking the deep and low position.

Jack and Elaine Doyle LaLanne — one of my exercise heroes!

Hand grippers — many to choose from, and I would find one that falls within your grip strength. This is an important exercise tool for working the nippers. The stronger your grip, the easier it will be to cut through tough hoof wall.

Recommended sit-up position. To avoid injury and sciatica, my recommendation is to keep the back flat on the supporting surface. From this position there are a surprising number of variations to go to. I've included a few here. I do all of these and more in my morning exercise. The bottom image at left is basically the "dying cockroach" position the Army drill instructors put us in daily for both "rewards and punishment." Work your way to this one, although few of us will be able to be as exemplary as the subject here. Just keep your legs up as high as you can. Hold it for a few seconds, then down with bent legs to rest, then up gain, etc. Progressive development will get you there. Patience!

Dumbbells

This is the last group of exercises I do. Their purpose is to strengthen and condition the arm, shoulder, and chest muscles. They really give you that "cut" look, too! The first question is, what weight dumbbell does one use? The rule I go by is select the maximum weight you can comfortably and safely control through an entire set of reps. Follow the images (#1 thru #5) as I explain what to do.

#1 demonstrates the alternating bicep curl; #2, the two arm curl. Notice that both subjects have their wrist/palms facing towards their bodies in the pre-lift, lower position. This is the most common position for most people based on human anatomy. Confirm that is applies to you as follows: without holding the weights, let both of your arms and hands hang loosely down at rest at your sides. Typically, the palms are facing towards your body and slightly rearward. If this is the case, then this is their natural starting position for holding the weights.

Next, raise the dumbbells so them so your palms are facing towards your body as the two subjects are doing. Depending on your upper arm conformation and musculature development, the dumbbells will either terminate at a slightly oblique (#1) or level (#2) angle. Lower them back down. In either case, you'll notice that as you raise and lower your arms, they rotate away from and towards their resting positions, respectively.

You may be asking why I'm not recommending barbells or weight machines. Barbells take up more space and are more limited than dumbbells in how weight

There are different variations that are possible here. These are the ones I do: (*3a*) pulling upwards from the front and (*3b*) from the side. In either case the movement is supported by bending forward slightly, which activates the abdominal muscles, which, in turn brings the full power of the lower and upper body muscle groups. I will do one set alternating the dumbbells, the other at the same time.

can be manipulated with our arms and hands. The same goes with weight machines. For our purposes, neither are needed anyway. Arnold Schwarzenegger wrote in one of his body building books that he didn't like using weight machines because they cramped the natural movements of his body, including his arms, wrists, and hands. I agree. I also find barbells very restrictive for doing curls, and wouldn't recommend them either for exercises #1 and #2.

Okay, as an additional exercise, go back to your basic push-up position and notice how you naturally position your hands on the floor. You'll probably find them rotated slightly inward, depending on your unique conformation. If so, that's your starting and ending position. It should feel natural and comfortable. If you're feeling any undue torsion (twist) on your wrists, you've not found your natural position. All this detail I had to scrutinize in order to do these power moves. And in each instance, I was seeking out my natural wrist, hand, arm and body positions and their corresponding trajectories. One doesn't just do these things, one figures them out. And, I would add, your overall sense of balance is also germane — meaning finding your center of gravity.

After completing the alternating curl (#1), I switch to #3a (*above*) an alternating

lift, doing 20 reps. From that I move directly to #4a, the alternating press, completing another 20 reps. As is always the case when beginning any of these exercises, examine any tendency for your wrist to rotate and follow that movement — do this first without the dumbbell to confirm, then with them.

After completing the alternating left/right arm sequence (#1→ #3a → #4a), rest briefly and then do the two arm sequence (#2→ #3b → #4b) with 20 reps each. These variant sequences compel the body to work differently, thus adding new dimensions to your strength and muscle mass.

This brings us to #5 (*next page*), which I used to develop my chest muscles for the still rings, facilitating the Iron Cross and other power moves. But the same muscles can be brought to bear when using the nippers. As I squeeze the nipper handles together with my hands, I simultaneously contract my arm and chest muscles which adds considerable more fire power to the gripping action. Try it and you'll see. Part of the action comes natural, but arguably a larger part is learned behavior.

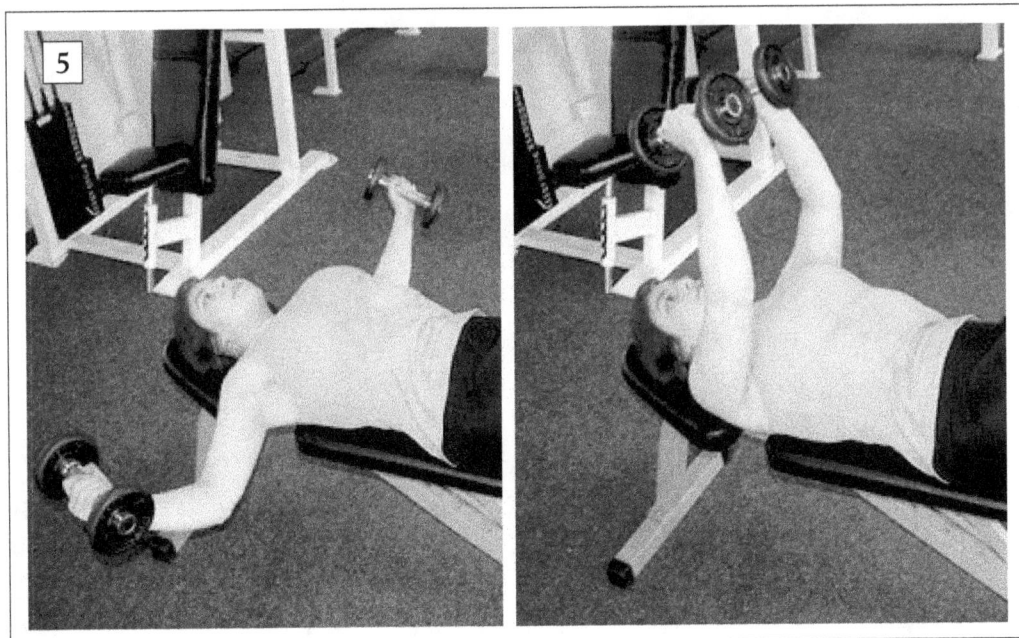

But be careful with this exercise! I do mine on the floor rather than on a workout bench (as is commonly done and depicted here), because there is less chance of the dumbbells pulling my arms down out of control. And because I also take the opportunity to do other dumbbell presses while on my back with intermittent sits ups. You can do this exercise with bent or straight arms. I do mine straight armed from habit as a gymnast. To avoid injury to your shoulder and arms, start with a weight that you can easily control, and do fewer reps to begin, and build from there.

I do one set of 20 reps (do two sets of 10 reps if that works better for you), with a short break followed by 20 reps each of #4a and #4b type presses at shoulder's width, also on my back. In addition to these, I do 20 more reps of a #2 type curl with my arms stretched to the sides bending at the elbow (upper arms laying flat) to do the curl. Together, these are a great power builder, but stay within your body's strength limits.

There are other floor and standing power moves I also do to finish, but they are all variants of the foregoing, and you can figure these out creatively as I have done, after confirming these basics.

Ladder climb

Here's another good one, if you don't have ready access to stairs or a hillside for your daily 20 minute "power walk." If you have space, get an 8 ft. ladder and climb up (for stability, just part way up) and down, repeating to create suitable

reps based on progressive development. If you over do it, you'll have aching arches — they'll recover, but in the meantime not fun! This exercise will strengthen the arches of your feet, the calves, thighs, and hips.

Start or end of the day walk/jog/bike

The workout routine above keeps you inside that 8 x 8 ft. space in your living room (or wherever). To balance that, I walk/jog for just 20 minutes. If you're going to walk, walk like a soldier on a forced march, meaning dig your heels in and really move along. Not a time for sauntering and lollygagging! If there's a nearby hill or other natural incline, preferably steep, incorporate that too — and you won't need the ladder. But whether walking, jogging, biking, or climbing a ladder, this is no time for procrastination, get off the sofa and get going!

§

In all of these exercises, I don't stop to take lengthy breaks, only long enough to sip water, a few seconds, which I do throughout the routine. So, it's pretty much non-stop, but never at a "killer pace." Jack LaLanne advocated for the continuous (non-stop), fluid integration of exercises, which I obviously fully embrace. Your "study assignment" here then is to move quickly to create and act on your 30 minute exercise regimen. These exercises will condition you for the work ahead under and around the horses in your care. You will do great!

The Natural Horse
Lessons From the Wild

The Natural Horse Quiz Key

1. With the help of the BLM, Jackson studied two samples of 125 Great Basin wild horses, totaling 1,000 sets of front/hind hooves. *True* (p. 2; p. 108, Table 6-1)

2. The facility where I measured most of the hooves of captured horses is known as the Litchfield Corrals, located twenty miles east of Susanville, California. *True* (p. 4) **I also measure hooves at the Burn's, OR and Palomino Valley, NV corrals.**

3. When I wrote *The Natural Horse* in the late 1980s I was still a farrier. *True* (p. 7) **But more than dubious about it. By 1990 I had ended my horseshoeing practice altogether.**

4. America's wild horses are feral horses, the offspring of domestic horses that have been turned loose, or escaped, into the wild. *True* (p. 9) **But "feral" is really a pejorative term to demean "wildness," equating wild to unruly and unkempt.**

5. Some time around 7,000 B.C. (late Pleistocene Epoch, "Ice Age"), the wild horse along with many other large land mammals, including the mammoth, mastodon, and sabertooth tiger, vanished from the North American continent. Not until 9,000 years later were they first reintroduced by Spanish conquistadores. *True* (pp. 11 and 13). **There are some who claim that *Equus ferus ferus* survived in North America and continued to live with Native Americans (Indians). But the only evidence in this regard is that early North American tribes contributed to their extinction by hunting them along with other predators.**

6. By the early 1800s, eyewitnesses estimated America's wild horse population at 2 to 5 million. *True* (p. 14). **But this is more anecdotal than based on credible evidence. I personally believe the numbers were much smaller based on French and Spanish explorers and colonialists who did not record such numbers in their encounters as early as the 1700s. The first apparent diffusion of horses "into the wild" occurred in the wake of the 1690 Pueblo Revolt in New Mexico. Plains Indians immediately began sweeping up such horses both to domesticate, trade, and eat. The Sioux and other Northern Plains didn't gain horses until the late 1700s, even with well-establish intertribal trading. Modern historians will need to revisit this subject.**

7. Not long before I entered wild horse country in 1982, no more than 50,000 wild horses were left on the open ranges due to the encroachments of civilization. Congress had passed two laws to protect wild horses from total eradication. Public Law 86-234, also known as the Wild Horse Annie Act — named after Velma Johnston, one of its principal supporters — passed in 1959. It prohibited the capture or destruction of wild horses using inhumane methods. Public Law 92-195, the Wild, Free-Roaming Horse and Burro Act, was passed in 1971; this put all wild horses under the administration of the U.S. Bureau of Land Management (BLM). *False* (pp. 15 and 26) **They are also administered by the U.S. Department of Forestry.**

8. According to a BLM public affairs official, "Calvary mounts, work horses and escaped or abandoned saddle animals from many breeds have all contributed to the wild horse's lineage . . . only a few descended from Spanish blood." *True* (p. 16) **DNA studies were not existent when the BLM published this. More research is needed.**

9. To be perfectly clear, the mustang, Equus caballus, Equus ferus caballus, and Equus ferus ferus are the same species and are genetically indistinguishable from each other. Only lifestyle and environment distinguish the horse living in the wild from the one living in human captivity. *True* (p. 17) **Read the Kirkpatrick paper on this subject posted on the AANHCP website and in the ISNHCP online library of learning materials.**

10. Most horse families are composed of a single dominant stallion, the *monarch*, and a closely guarded *harem* of females with whom he bonds and breeds. *True* (p. 19)

11. Great Basin lands that are home to its wild horses are similar. Typically, there are mountains (5,000 to 10,000 feet), small buttes (mesas), gently rolling hills, and broad alluvial plains. Rocks and boulders are scattered everywhere. The plains, where natural, are normally a mixture of firm soil and soft sand, interspersed with small volcanic rocks and a myriad of plant life and grasses. *True* (p. 26)

12. *Home range* can be defined as any area where a band, or assembly of related bands, happens to take up residence in order to exact their survival needs. The size and shape of the home range is not fixed, as though an invisible fence were in place. *True* (p. 27)

13. Wild horse territorial behavior is exhibited by the presence of "stud piles" — fairly large piles of dung, some as high as two to three feet — excreted by various bands occupying the same rangeland. *True* (p. 28)

14. The basic elements of the *natural gait complex* — the hereditary locomotive archetype of *Equus ferus caballus* * — results from specific behaviors that are routine and uniform across all of wild horse society. *True* (p. 31) **This is to say that nature evolved the anatomy of the horse to facilitate the types of behaviors essential to the survival of the species.**

15. *Collection* is essentially a centering or balancing process that is natural to the horse. *True* (p. 32)

16. We should try to understand the mechanics of natural movement within the context of the behaviors that produce it so uniformly across wild horse society. *True* (p. 33) **Most students will probably avoid studying this material until such time that they stare the brutality of equine lameness in the face as NHC practitioners.**

17. The hooves of the horse are like little mirrors that reflect back upon the animal's entire locomotive experience. In this way, they are visible, tangible repositories of knowledge of lifestyle. *True* (p. 35) **Although the text specifies the Great Basin wild horse, it applies to the lifestyle (experience) of any horse.**

18. The *Natural Gait Complex* refers specifically to the horse's *footfall sequences, leads, stride and stride extension, rhythm, tempo, cadence, and suspension*. *True* (p. 36) **All of this is very important — see my comment on Q16.**

19. The leading or initiating hind leg is pivotal in many ways to the natural locomo-

tion of the horse. Not only does it mark the first step, or footfall, of a stride . . . but it is the leg upon which the horse initiates changes in lead, direction of travel, body extension or contraction, gait, tempo, speed, and collection. *True* (p. 44) **This statement, as you have read in the book, contradicts virtually every equestrian expert's take on leads. But it is the natural gait complex that has the final word, in my opinion.**

20. *Collection* represents a distinct change in the temperament, poise, body posture, and locomotive style of the horse from the ordinary to the extraordinary. *True* (p. 45) **But, my opinion, suggested more than once in the book, is that collection ceases to be collection when it is forced by the rider.**

21. The corollary between altering stride extension and cadence amid constant tempo and rhythm — resulting in changes in speed — has been an important focus among many of the world's finest riders and trainers. *True* (p. 46-47)

22. Xenophon wrote that collection is not something that can be forced upon the horse. It is a state of mind and body in which the horse engages willfully due to specific behavioral stimuli. *True* (p. 49) **So true, and worth never forgetting.**

23. Collection is innate to the animal, who knows when, where, to what extent, and how to collect themselves. *True* (p. 65) **The horse doesn't need us to teach it either.**

24. The natural hoof is uniform in terms of its fundamental front and hind shapes throughout wild horse society, but it is also uniquely endowed with endless subtle variations in angle, size, and color (pigmentation or absence of) that set the hooves of one horse off from those of another. *True* (p. 70)

25. Averages and ranges are included for a few of the dozen or so measurement categories I sampled. Hind hooves, on average, are slightly smaller than front hooves. *True* (p. 70) **Here, you should be asking yourself, how are they smaller?**

26. Not surprising, overall hoof size increased directly with a horse's age until about age five. *True* (p. 72) **Now explain why this happened.**

27. Basically, I found three hoof color schemes: yellowish to whitish light-colored hooves lacking pigmentation; striated and mottled hooves with various combinations of black pigmentation and no pigmentation; and all black pigmented hooves. *True* (p. 72) **Now explain what the impact of pigmentation has on the horse's hooves.**

28. The angle of growth of the hoof wall is steeper at the toe than at the heel — the grain is not parallel from toe to heel. (T/F) *True* (p. 73)

29. The term *wall bevel*, in spite of its common usage among farriers and some horse enthusiasts, is probably misleading. *True* (p. 73) **Why is it misleading?**

30. Although I examined hooves in both winter and summer, it was never clear whether frogs underwent a molting process or were kept constantly trim as a result of locomotive wear. *True* (p. 76) **What did I learn about this from Paddock Paradise that confirmed my thinking in one direction?**

31. The frog, frog stay, and digital cushion serve to help brace the hoof during support while mitigating associated concussional shock waves coming upwards from ground impact. *True* (p. 77) **Farriers hold that these structures, citing the frog in particular, act as "blood pump"— driving circulation throughout the hoof;**

NHC science holds that it is the weight-bearing force that drives circulation as explained later in this book (p. 84, "Hoof Mechanism").

32. The volar profile — the bottom of the hoof — is recessed in distinct gradations from one structure to the next. *True* (p. 79) **Make sure you can name them!**

33. I found that two hooves with the same heel length and identical toe lengths could have entirely different toe angles. *True* (p. 81) **Explain how this happens.**

34. *Hoof symmetry* refers to the correspondence in size, form, and arrangement of structures or parts of the hoof on opposite sides of the hoof's *median plane*. *True* (p. 83) **Give an example of how *hoof asymmetry* is different.**

35. The NHC hoof mechanism is a simplified model that explains the naturally balanced hoof's changes as it passes through its flight and support phases. *True* (p. 84) **How does the NHC model differ from the conventional model?**

36. Areas of active and passive wear are not carved into the hoof by the natural hoof care practitioner — they emerge and recede respectively as a consequence of natural movement. *True* (p. 88) **Can you explain where these areas of active wear are located on the bottom of the hoof?**

37. Little is known radiographically about the wild horse hoof. *True* (p. 92) **But what do we know from radiographs of my wild horse biospecimens?**

38. Heel growth naturally occurs at a slower rate than at the toe. *False* (p. 94) **Why is it thought to grow faster at the heels?**

39. P3 is a non-weight bearing structure. *True* (p. 96) **This statement is considered outlandish and unproven. My opinion is the opposite is true.**

40. Nature selects for a broad range of physical and temperamental types, all of which appear to be perfectly suitable for a rugged life in the wild. Variation is clearly nature's way. *True* (p. 102) **A true "lesson from the wild."**

41. The principal idea behind generating naturally shaped hooves in the domestic horse is simple: to help the animal move in the way that nature intended. *True* (p. 107) **And such a simple idea, painfully abused.**

42. Hoof measurements are arguably the most important part of the natural trim method, which is why we call them the *Critical Measurements*. *True* (p. 109)

43. The HMR uses the SP (support plane) to determine the hoof's VP (volar plane). *True* (p. 109) **But this does not necessarily equate to "hoof balance."**

44. *Nipper dragging* is a unique technique for removing excess sole growth. *True* (p. 110) **Spending as much time practicing dragging on cadavers cannot be over emphasized.**

45. The sole dermis (growth corium) extrudes layer upon layer of sheets of epidermis called *solar plates*. *True* (p. 110)

46. Nipper "runs" commence at the toe because starting at the heels runs the risk of unbalancing the heel buttresses. *True* (p. 111) **Make this a habit when trimming.**

47. A distinct widening of the medial toe wall typically corresponds to a natural *support pillar*. *True* (p. 111)

48. The midline of the volar profile is technically known in NHC as the *Medial Axis of the Volar Profile* ("MAVP"). *True* (p. 112) **You will use this Navigational Land-**

mark again and again.

49. The *Mediolateral Heel Axis* ("MLHA") is used when sighting the back of the hoof to balance the heels. *True* (p. 112) **Use the Hoof Balancer Tool to train your eye to see this axis.**

50. The Mustang Roll technically is a biodynamic growth pattern that we facilitate through precision trimming and natural boarding. *True* (p. 112) **But explain also what is meant by "biodynamic."**

51. Setting the nipper blade at the juncture of the *s. medium* with the *s. internum* facilitates the most important cut of the Mustang Roll. *True* (p. 113) **This will require considerable practice.**

52. The Mustang Roll includes all the strata of the hoof wall and the *s. lamellatum.* *True* (p. 113) **Name all the strata using their technical names.**

53. Also critical to the Mustang Roll is that the nipper cut leave the *s. lamellatum* active (distal) to the contiguous sole, but passive (proximal) to the *s. internum*. *True* (p. 114) **Think about this statement as you evaluate the structures involved.**

54. There are no accessible "flat" surfaces in the naturally shaped volar profile to rasp. *True* (p. 115) **Hard to believe give the obsession with farriers to flatten out the bottom of the hoof!**

55. The natural biodynamic response of the Mustang Roll includes a rim of protruding *s. internum* that extends to the entire distal periphery of the capsule, including the heel buttresses and the bars whose turns form the seats-of-corn. *True* (p. 116) **Nothing to ignore, and worth looking at with horses that are barefoot whenever the opportunity presents itself to you.**

56. Excess growth, in the NHC interpretation, is actually different than what is commonly referred to as "flare." *Flare* is a common, but unnatural, growth pattern seen in domesticated horse populations today. It is characterized by a weakened hoof wall that typically "bends" outwards. *True* (p. 118) **When you reach the cadaver phase of your training, evaluate hooves so that you know the difference. Flare is so ingrained in the mentality of horse owners, this can be tough to overcome.**

57. The wear line is the upper extent of the roll on the outer wall, and is very distinct in the wild horse hoof. *True* (p. 121)

58. "Walking the hoof stand" means encircling the hoof while it is stabilized on the grip head of the hoof stand. *True* (p. 121) **I recommend that you practice this away from the horse. You'll get dizzy at first, don't want you falling into the horse!**

59. Bringing the outermost edge of the *s. internum* just into view is a critical step in pre-forming the Mustang Roll. *True* (p. 122) **Like I write, teach the horse's owner to help out with this.**

60. The trimmer's "deep and low" stance works well with the horse's anatomy, and the animal readily accommodates it. *True* (p. 123) **Which of the 5 Basic Positions in Sequencing does the trimmer use "deep and low?"**

61. The HB-1 (Hoof Buffer) is the final tool used to complete the natural trim. *True* (p. 124) **The HB-2 was used but had to be discontinued as the manufacturer was unable to replicate the cutting surface.**

62. The outer layers of the frog separate from the hoof in a similar way that solar plates leave the sole. *True* (p. 126) **At some point you will run into this in your practice with horses new to NHC.**

63. The *Hoof Balancer Tool* is used in two ways: 1) As a sighting instrument for balancing the heels; 2) As an overlay upon the volar profile of the hoof for determining the location of the support triad. *True* (p. 128) **In fact, it's the alignment of sighting the hoof in both planes that leads to hoof balance.**

64. The 5 Basic Positions of Sequencing taught in the ISNHCP Natural Trim Training Program are an amalgamation of techniques I learned many years ago as a farrier, what I learned from wild and domesticated horses, innovations that coincided with the development of new tools and equipment, and the requirements of the natural trim itself to do it correctly in keeping with the wild horse model. *True* (p. 130)

65. Sequencing involves all parts of the trimming process except the trim itself. *True* (p. 130) **Practically an oxymoron!**

66. "Paddock Paradise" is a concept for natural horse boarding borne of the wild horse lifestyle in the U.S. Great Basin. *True* (p. 135) **After pushing this for years, along with many others, it's hard to believe that relatively few horse owners are aware of Paddock Paradise.**

67. Technically, laminitis occurs as a pathological separation of the hoof from the horse. *True* (p. 159) **Arguably the best definition of laminitis!**

68. *Lamina* or *laminae* (plural) refers to the network of dermal and epidermal leaf-like structures that interlock together (called "interdigitation") to form a complex bridge of connective tissue between the inner hoof wall and the outer face of the lowermost bone of the horse's foot. Collectively, these laminae form the *s. lamellatum*. *True* (p. 160) **This can get a bit confusing, because we distinguish between the epidermal and dermal leaves, but also the primary and secondary epidermal leaves. For our purposes the descending PELs represent the s. lamellatum, while all the epidermal and dermal leaves constitute the lamellar attachment mechanism (LAM), also called the lamellar suspensory apparatus which NHC science contests as being a bogus concept.**

69. Laminitis is not limited to the laminae of the hoof, for separation of the hoof from the horse also occurs across the sole, frog, or wherever the hoof might be attached to the horse's foot. *True* (p. 161) **So true, but seldom acknowledged, at least not until the entire hoof falls off of a severely stricken laminitic horse.**

70. The *laminitis zone* is technically referred to as the *lamellar attachment mechanism* ("LAM"). It is here that laminitis occurs. *True* (p. 161) **But, with the understanding explained in Q69 above.**

71. The *basement membrane* is a thin membranous sheet of tough connective tissue. *True* (p. 162)

72. When we apply the principles and proven practices of *natural horse care* ("NHC") based on the wild, free-roaming horse of the Great Basin, healing — and preventing — laminitis is facilitated through basic and relatively straightforward changes in how we manage our horses. *True* (p. 168) **On this point we equate "healing" and "prevention" in dealing with laminitis.**

The Natural Trim
Basic Guidelines

Basic Guidelines Quiz Key

1. Unnatural lifestyles create unnaturally shaped hooves, no matter how precise the natural trim. ***True. p. 7.*** **Explain why in terms of biodynamics discussed in** ***The Natural Horse.***

2. In 2010, fate provided me with the opportunity to create a Paddock Paradise, replete with horses trimmed only by me. The natural trim would be put to the test and I would see the results before my very eyes. ***True. p. 7.***

3. It became unmistakably clear to me that it was the "wildness" of our horses' hooves that left the indelible impression of consternation on visitors' faces. ***True. p. 8.***

4. I have come to realize that wildness can be a formidable barrier to understanding transformative events in the conscious mind that is saturated with, and only knows, domestication. ***True. p. 8.***

5. Paddock Paradise, as I had hoped, breeched the barrier between wildness and domestication. But, in so doing, created a new abstraction, a void fraught with a steady stream of blank human faces. ***True. p. 9.*** **I believe the word "abstraction" is the key issue to try to understand. As one begins to "see" and experience the results of NHC, one should not expect others to see the same thing as you.**

6. The natural trim, in my mind, had, in fact, metamorphosed from basic trim mechanics into a "chess game" of complex biodynamic responses to what I did to the hoof. If I did such and such, what would the response be? ***True. p. 9.*** **At some point, one begins to anticipate certain results, later it goes without saying that a specific outcome is, in fact, going to happen or can't, depending on circumstances.**

7. The hoof is biologically equipped to work with us, or fail in the worst of ways. ***True. p. 10.*** **If one expects otherwise, one will be disappointed.**

8. One does not force the foot to look like a wild horse hoof, but simply facilitates its growth through the natural trim method. ***True. p. 11.*** **Explain in one short sentence how the natural trim facilitates this natural growth pattern.**

9. We use the wild horse hoof as our model simply because both the wild horse and their hooves are the pictures of equine health and soundness. ***True. p. 11.***

10. I still find it hard to believe that, until I conducted my wild horse research literally thousands of years after the first horse was domesticated, the scientific basis for the "natural trim" has been both unpublished and unknown. ***True. p. 12.***

11. My wild horse hoof research findings were first presented in 1988 at the Annual Conference of the American Farriers Association in Lexington, Kentucky (USA). ***True. p. 12.***

12. The *Basic Guidelines* are used when hooves are healthy and not suffering from extreme deformity due to chronic laminitis, criminal neglect, and hoof care

methods which force the hoof into unnatural, if not pathological, shapes and sizes. ***True. p. 13.***

13. The evolutionary descent of *E. ferus caballus* through natural selection brings with it a powerful, although unseen, force embedded in the animal's DNA. In NHC science, we call this the adaptation force (or simply the A-force). ***True. p. 13.* In fact, it is this force that facilitates healings through complex changes in hoof mass.**

14. It is entirely plausible that Global Warming caused a retreat of glaciers in the late Pleistocene Epoch that spawned fructan-rich grasses in their wake that many ungulates (hoofed animals) including the horse could not digest. This metabolic incapacitation led to unprecedented levels of a debilitating and life-threatening disease NHC science defines as Whole Horse Inflammatory Disease (WHID). ***True. p. 14.* Researchers have discovered earlier Ice Age events that resolved with horses perishing from WHID.**

15. WHID expresses itself symptomatically throughout the horse's body as a range of bodily disorders, such as colic, abnormal hair growth, cancer, organ failure, inflammation of the feet resulting in lameness. ***True. p. 14.* Explain how horses then became extinct due to WHID.**

16. I had presented 30 freeze-dried wild horse hoof biospecimens at the 1988 American Farriers Association Annual Conference. All who came by my table agreed: the hooves were peculiar looking, were not balanced, and badly needed correction! ***True. p. 17.* What was my explanation for this perception by the farriers? Because it is likely you will face the same thing one day yourself.**

17. Today, trained NHC practitioners like myself understand that the range of outcomes produced by the natural trim correspond directly with the faithfulness with which horse owners embrace and act upon the other 3 Pillars. ***True. p. 17.* This is extremely important information for your mental health, because you don't want to take personal responsibility for others shortcomings.**

Note: Pages 18-25 were introduced to you in *The Natural Horse*. This is incredibly important information to go through carefully as it is foundational to the Navigational Landmarks from which the Critical Measurements are derived. It may be helpful to return to *The Natural Horse* and contrast the discussions.

18. A deeper knowledge of the structures of the horse's foot and related biology really only comes into play when tackling the problems associated with upper body trauma and diseases resulting in extreme capsule deformity. ***True. p. 27.* Increasingly, my thinking is that this level of work should take place with full veterinary support that integrates seamlessly with NHC methods and science.**

19. An important distinction should be made between the oft heard terms "hoof, capsule, and foot." Hoof and capsule are synonymous. They correspond to the outer or epidermal parts (epidermis : outer skin that lacks nerves and blood vessels) of the horse's foot that we can see and touch. The horse's "foot," in contrast, refers to all of the epidermal parts and its contents. ***True. p. 27.* Equally important to know the is interface between the two (e.g., the LAM).**

20. The parts of the capsule are *biodynamic*, meaning they are capable of changing

their location, mass, and angle of growth. *True. p. 27.* **The perception that this is not true stems from the widespread acceptance of farrier science and methods that obstruct or corrupt capsule biodynamics.**

21. The outer hoof wall is comprised of the toe, quarter, and heel; these artificial divisions are only approximations. *True. p. 28.*

22. As a farrier, I was taught that the toe wall and the heel both grow at the same angle; this is an entrenched farrier mythology disproved by the wild horse model. *True. p. 28.*

23. The wear line of the Mustang Roll circumscribes the entire hoof wall, approximately 1 cm above ground level (i.e., the Support Plane, "SP"). *True. p. 28.* **This constitutes another "lesson from the wild," so apparent to the NHC practitioner faced with a myriad of unnaturally worn hooves in domestication.**

24. The epidermal structures of the foot's volar profile include the ground-bearing surface of the hoof wall, sole, and frog. *True. p. 29.*

25. The *hard sole plane* (HSP) is virtually unseen and, therefore, unknown in domestication because, unlike in the wild or in a PP that simulates that adaptive environment, it is invariably removed by excessive trimming or being shrouded in excess growth (i.e., solar plates). *True. p. 30.* **This is something you will inevitably see around you with horses living in captivity and no access to NHC.**

26. The tendency, if not the practice, of hoof care professionals is to trim the frog until its "flaps" are removed. This constitutes a violation of the Basic Guidelines because, as the wild horse model reveals here, the flaps are intended to be there, in tact, as part of the hoof's epidermal armor. *True. p. 30.* **Obsession with frog "tidiness" lies at the bottom of this. Trimming of the frog is indicated when it breeches the Mediolateral Heel Axis (MLHA).**

27. The *digital cushion* is a fibro-fatty structure lying above (proximal to) the frog. Its posterior salience blends with the subcutaneous tissues of the skin and periople to form the heel bulbs. The frog provides epidermal armor for the digital cushion. *True. p. 30.* **Use the Step 2 cadaver trim clinic to open this part of the hoof to see these relationships.**

28. The *s. tectorium, s. medium, s. internum,* and *s. lamellatum* collectively form the Mustang Roll. *True. p. 31* (Figure 3-3b). **But with the understanding that we are talking specifically about the epidermal lamellae of the *s. lamellatum* and intertubular horn extruded by the terminal papillae (Figure 3-22) during the bonding of the *s. lamellatum* with the epidermal sole.**

29. The bones of the horse's <u>foot</u> include the cannon bone, splint bones, sessamoid bones, long and short pastern bones, coffin bone, and the navicular bone. *True. p. 32.* **This is often comes as a surprise as we are accustomed to thinking of the hoof as the foot!**

30. While there is considerable emphasis placed on the alignment of the bones of the digit (P1, P2, and P3) among farriers, vets, and even generic (don't follow the wild horse model) barefoot trimmers, this is of little or no interest to the NHC practitioner who simply trims the hoof. *True. p. 32.* **So, why would I say such a thing?**

31. There are two major tendons acting upon the horse's foot, the *deep digital flexor*

tendon (DDFT) and the *common digital extensor tendon* (CDET). ***True. p. 34.***

32. The actions of the DDFT and CDET upon the bones and joints are complex as the foot moves through its support and flight phases (recall Table 3-4 in *The Natural Horse*). While interesting from a biomechanical standpoint, they are not germane to the natural trim, which, by definition, facilitates the natural actions of all these structures, whatever they might be, by default. ***True. p. 34.* While this statement is technically correct when confined to trimming, I used this information to deduce and confirm the 5 Basic Positions used in Sequencing.**

[Note to student: from page 36 to page 43 addresses the birth of the capsule. This is an extremely important part of your education and is deserved of much time and study.]

33. While one can distinguish the hoof wall corium from the sole corium, frog corium, and other coria, NHC science treats all the foot's coria as a single, integrated body called the Supercorium. ***True. p. 36.* This is important to understand as there is cell to cell communication going on in the foot that is integral to healing mass changes.**

34. If [the hoof is] not shod or subjected to unnatural management practices, all epidermal armor manufactured by the Supercorium is subject to natural and well-orchestrated mass changes that may occur simultaneously anywhere at any time across the entire hoof . . . such changes operate outside current published farriery and veterinary models of the shod hoof. ***True. p. 36.* This relates to Q33 above.**

35. In effect, the hoof wall is actually hair cemented together. ***True. p. 37.* Interesting fact that even surprised me — 45 years ago!**

36. I believe the rise of "corrective shoeing" can be attributed to unresponsive pathological hoof growth patterns. ***True. p. 38.* This also relates to Q33 above.**

37. Like other coria of the Supercorium, the sole corium is highly vascularized and contributes to intracapsular hydraulic forces of the hoof mechanism ***True. p. 42.* (see Chapter 6).**

38. While the sole and frog support weight-bearing forces, it is also true that, relative to SP, those same weight-bearing forces are going to concentrate more over the hoof wall because — in the naturally shaped hoof — neither the sole nor the frog endure direct contact with SP. ***True. p. 44.* This is taken up further in *The Natural Trim: Principles and Practice* in the chapter dealing with the "Hoof Mechanism." Very important information and integral to natural hoof form and function.**

39. Close examination reveals that only one stratum of the hoof wall makes contact with SP: the *s. internum* . . . . One could argue, of course, that, in life, the entire bottom of the hoof endures ground contact. True! But, the fact remains, weight-bearing forces always seek out the most immediate path to the ground. ***True. p. 44.* Relates to Q38 above.**

40. Relative concavity is as follows across the volar profile, beginning with the Mustang Roll: *s. tectorium* is proximal to *s. medium*, which is proximal to *s. internum*, which is distal to the *s. lamellatum*, which is distal to the sole, which is distal to

the frog. *True. p. 44.* **Use Figure 3-25 to help clarify these relationships in your mind. Enough to make one dizzy!**

41. H° is important because it tells us about the stability or instability of the hoof relative to its natural state (N°). *True. p. 46.* **H° is our direct link to the wild horse model; hence, this is a foundational focus in your training at the hoof.**

42. Hooves suffering from unnatural care practices will reveal shifts in H° – called migrations – away from the natural ranges for N°. *True. p. 46.*

43. H° exists in a mysterious tug of war between its ancestral A-force and the contemporaneous effects of domestication. *True. p. 47.* **Typically, this represents, if not an area of confusion for the student, an opening for not applying H° seriously in their work. But the ancestral A-force is as real and operative as anything else in the animal's life. Our job is to reconcile it with H° in our work.**

44. Knowing where H° is going, and why, is our challenge as NHC practitioners. Our goal is for H° to settle, accompanied by the soundness and vitality of the horse. *True. p. 47.* **This is the A-force acting on the hoof per Q43.**

45. The *Critical Measurements* are important because they are based on the theory of H° – and, thus, connect us directly to the wild horse model – and because they guide us safely through the natural trim by enabling "safe cuts" to the millimeter and single degree accuracy. *True. p. 48.* **Here, H° as a utility available to us, expands in its influence to all other Critical Measurements.**

46. The Support Plane (SP) is any level surface that can support the horse's hoof; the Volar Plane (VP) corresponds to the points of the hoof wall pressing against the SP. *True. p. 49.* **Thus it is said the SP defines VP. But, once more, it does not necessarily equate to hoof balance.**

47. The *Navigational Landmarks* are very specific lines drawn on the hoof relative to certain structures that are common to all equine hooves. There are eight such landmarks used in the Basic Guidelines. *True. p. 50 and Figure 5-3.* **You should be asking here, from what or where are these landmarks derived?**

48. The landmarks are derived from a 3 dimensional spatial grid, called the *Hoof Plexus*. This is an abstract network of horizontal and perpendicular lines, points, planes, and angles that facilitate the measuring of hoof size, proportion, and growth angles – the *Critical Measurements* – based on the theory of H°. *True. p. 50 and Figure 5-4.* **So, Q48 answers Q47. This is an invitation to study the Hoof Plexus and then use it as a reference as necessary in your study and applications of the theory of H°.**

49. There are many *Critical Measurements* derived from the Hoof Plexus, but only two are used in the Basic Guidelines. These are very specific measurements for toe angle (H°) and toe length (H°TL) that are unique to natural hoof care based on the wild horse model. *True. p. 50.* **The other measurements referred to are used in fitting hoof boots, monitoring de-contractional changes in hooves following de-shoeing, diagnosing clubfoot in Navicular Syndrome, and with more complex applications of the Advanced Guidelines.**

50. There are two additional Critical Measurements of interest, B° and B°TL. These measurements are corollaries of H° and H°TL, arising from capsule deformity due to pathology. Technically, however, they are the providence of the Advanced Guidelines. *True. p. 52.*

51. All hoof mapping begins with the Median Axis of the Volar Profile (MAVP). *True. p. 54.* **The MAVP enables us to determine the MATW, and from there, H° and H°TL.**

[Note to student: from this point forward — pages 54 to 64 — is your introduction to gridding the hooves for the Navigational Landmarks and then determining values for H° and H°TL. This will be the primary focus of your Step 2 Clinic; thus, spending considerable time here studying these pages is highly recommended to prepare you for the hand's-on applications with your clinician. Practicing on the front hooves of your own horse/s is also recommended.]

52. The MAVP-MATW Joint ("MM-Joint") connects the volar and mediolateral profiles of the hoof in such a way as to set the stage for measuring H° and H°TL. *True. p. 54.* **This statement focuses more closely on the determination made in Q51.**

53. Technically, the MM-Joint joint occurs where the MATW is formed, namely at the juncture of the MAVP with the outer wall of the *s. medium* — or the *s. tectorium* if the latter is not worn or rasped away. *True. p. 54.* **This statement builds further on Q51, which is to say that in scribing the Navigational Landmarks, they are structure specific and not just lines randomly drawn up and down and across the capsule.**

54. The MATW is drawn in alignment with the "grain" of the hoof — i.e., the horn tubules visible in the s. medium. **True. p. 56. Still more information in gridding the MATW — the orientation of the horn tubules in the toe wall — thus we are building more focus yet on Q51.**

55. The bull's-eye (☉) is a single point on the face of the toe wall enabling us to find H°, H°TL, B° and B°TL. *True. p. 59.*

56. The MPTW is defined as an imaginary plane — think of a pane of glass but without any physical mass ("matterless mass")! — that passes through the bull's-eye and the entire hoof at a right angle (90°) to the SP. *True. p. 60.* **You may want to reference the Hoof Plexus to visualize it.**

57. To measure H°, the hoof's support pillars must all be placed on SP. *True. p. 64.* **Once again, this is not to imply that the hoof is naturally balanced. Only that H° can be measured in any hoof, no matter how deformed or imbalanced.**

58. B° and B°TL are two additional Critical Measurements that you should be aware of, as they are very likely to show up in most horses today due to the international epidemic of WHID. *True. p. 66.*

59. B° and B°TL are pathological corruptions of H° and H°TL. *True. p. 66.*

[Note to student: In addition to this quiz, take the Chapter 5 Quiz on pp. 71-72 in the Basic Guidelines; an answer key is provided at the back of the book.]

60. *Active* and *passive* wear are significant characteristics of the naturally shaped hoof. They represent the natural convolutions of the hoof wall's ground-bearing sur-

face. *True. p. 74.* But without other information derived from the Hoof Balancer Tool, or an experienced eye, we cannot say that the hooves are naturally balanced.

61. *Active wear* typically occurs in groups of 3 support pillars (medial toe wall and both heel-buttresses); these groups are also called support triads. *True. p. 74.*

62. SP is used to define VP. However, this does not mean that VP is naturally balanced, only that it has been located. More information is needed to define or make a determination of hoof balance. *True. p. 74.* Worth repeating because students commonly presume that the presence of triads equate to balanced hooves.

63. H°TL is the shortest possible length of the toe wall that can be trimmed without penetrating the HSP *True. p. 74.* It goes without saying, however, this statement is not true if H° has been incorrectly located and the Hoof Meter Reader (HMR) wasn't used to take the measurement.

64. The objective of *nipper dragging* is to expose the HSP from toe to heel-buttresses. *True. p. 78.*

65. *Frog notching* in conjunction with nipper dragging is an important and useful technique to confirm both the HSP and *heel length. True. p. 79.* Both notching and dragging are high priority exercises in your Step 2 clinic.

66. Balancing the heels sets the stage for balancing the entire hoof. *True. p. 80.* Very important because if the heels are not balanced relative to the MPVP, then this hoof is not balanced either by definition.

67. After the heels are balanced, the MLHA is determined (and, thus, the HFP), and the heel-buttresses are brought to their optimal length, the result is a balanced hoof relative to SP. *True. p. 82.* Let me restate this: the MLHA is determined and scribed using the Hoof Balancer Tool; the heels are then trimmed to the MLHA, and — assuming the triad is correct across the VP, the hoof is said to be naturally balanced. This assumes also that H°TL has been confirmed through nipper dragging and the HMR.

68. Mastery of the *Basic Guidelines* is crucial to understanding the *Advanced Guidelines*, and attempts to trim deformed hooves — the temptation of many beginners — without HTLA confirmed leads directly to invasive trimming. *True. p. 82.* I bring this up here because HTLA (H°TL Axis) can be really tricky to find in some deformed hooves (slippered and wried simultaneously). And without this Navigational Landmark pinpointed, the solar dome is vulnerable to being breeched.

69. If a horse is living in a stall, a walled paddock, or a grass pasture, the hooves given a natural trim will not be naturally balanced. Balanced? Artificially so, *possibly.* Naturally balanced? *Not at all. True. p. 84.* One cannot wish for something to be something that it isn't, settling for illusions. Either sufficient elements of the 4 Pillars have been introduced, or they haven't.

[Note to student: From page 88 to 90 lies the principal defense of horses going barefoot. The conventional argument for the "hoof mechanism" is that the horseshoe is needed to *protect and support* the hoof under the weight of the rider, if not the horse themselves going barefoot. Because the wild horse model is still rejected or ignored by mainstream veterinary science, it is the burden of the NHC practitioner to counter this misguided science. The NHC model for the hoof mechanism points not only to the reality of the wild horse, but to an entirely different premise of weight-bearing by the horse's foot. This discussion began in your studies of *The Natural Horse*, so review the same material here again to confirm your ability to defend the wild horse model.]

70. It is logical that *sequencing* should assume a core role in trimming horses, even though trimming per se is not defined by sequencing, nor vice versa. *True. p. 91.* **Again, sequencing is only concerned with efficient management of the horse and the tools/equipment used in trimming. For this reason, sequencing is taught independently of trimming, the latter added in once sequencing is confirmed.**

71. Efficiency during the natural trim means having the tools "homed" in the hoof stand — every tool has its own place on the stand and is kept there until used, and returned to its home once the task is completed. *True. p. 91.* **Tools scattered all over the place, whether on the ground or in the tool caddy, is a sure sign of incompetence.**

72. Relative dominance, or "RD" as I call it, refers to the horse's natural instinct to establish his position in the specie's pecking order. *True. p. 91.* **Thus, it goes without saying, RD is also a role we must assume in relating to horses.**

73. Sooner or later, most horses will "test" the trimmer by breaking sequence to see if they can control the situation, just as they would do in the wild. *True. p. 92.* **Most students new to NHC lose control of their horses when sequencing due to their assumption of Beta roles in RD. Fortunately, RD is something that can be taught and learned.**

74. My standard policy and recommendation is to not trim or have anything to do with abused horses. Our job is to trim, not rehabilitate traumatized animals. *True. p. 92.* **Taking on troubled horses by students is common across all hoof care disciplines. Shrewd and often dishonest horse owners who are abusive of their horses and refuse to learn natural horsemanship are always on the lookout to exploit neophytes. The ISNHCP teaches students how to determine which horses are troubled, and recommend strongly that their owners be declined as clients.**

75. Horses are incredibly perceptive and intelligent and know when you are playing them versus when you are sincere. They are also discriminating of competent and incompetent trimmers, but are likely to be more cooperative if they are rewarded for being patient! *True. p. 92.* **But not all horses are cooperative and will purposefully harm people they do not trust or fear. The student must confirm themselves to RD to prevent personal injury.**

76. To facilitate optimal understanding between our species, I use and teach two fundamental communication skills: "ear radar" and "pressuring the muscle ring." *True. p. 93.* **These are instruments of RD.**

77. The position and movement of the horse's ears reveals a lot about his feelings and behavior. This is called "ear radar." *True. p. 93.* **Worth repeating as ear radar is widely misunderstood and/or ignored.**

78. Ear radar and pressure points on the muscle ring connect into the specie's responsiveness based on relative dominance. Learning to read the horse's radar and apply pressure with discretion and praise/rewards will elevate the trimmer higher in the social hierarchy, commanding respect and cooperation. ***True. p. 95.*** **This statement builds further on Q77-78. Again, the objective of the trimmer is to gain, or at least feign, if possible, alpha status over the horse. Most horses are beta, including males, even stallions, so there is the element of "luck," but sending students out into the horse world not committed to RD is one of my greatest fears.**

79. Horses are very perceptive and discriminating, and will readily exploit to a lower position of relative dominance those trimmers who are not in shape and are struggling to sequence. This can mean different things, all of them unpleasant. ***True. p. 96.*** **Less of a focus on RD, more about the necessity of incorporating exercise in one's work as an NHC practitioner. For this reason, I've include a chapter on exercises that I've personally used for over 60 years, and still do daily to this day. ISNHCP Field Instructors may decline mentorships to any student who is out of shape and at risk of personal injury as a result.**

80. Battles between horses and farriers are legend in the horse world, virtually all of it unnecessary when the principles of sequencing are understood, confirmed, and practiced. Barefooters are not exempt from such outcomes either. ***True. p. 96.*** **This is why it is taught and enforced in the ISNHCP training program. Students not confirmed to sequencing cannot advance to the Field Mentorships.**

81. The *support diagonals* are derived from the specie's natural gait complex (NGC) and, therefore, are readily assumed by the horse when commanded by the trimmer (or Handler) using RD. ***True. p. 96.*** **The diagonals are truly a gift from nature!**

82. The *5 Basic Positions* are an amalgamation of techniques I learned many years ago as a farrier, what I learned later from wild and domesticated horses, innovations that coincided with the development of new tools and equipment, and the requirements of the natural trim itself to do it correctly in keeping with the wild horse model. ***True. p. 98.*** **It is true that much has gone into the development of these positions over many years. However, they are nearly useless to the student who fails to exercise their bodies as recommend in this training manual.**

83. "Deep and low" is used in all positions, wherein the trimmer can brace their elbows on their thighs for work, rest, and relieving the lower back of stress during trimming. ***True. p. 98.*** **If it weren't for deep/low I would have quit this work decades ago. Let me rephrase this: nature would have put me out of work decades ago.**

84. Because of the orderliness of sequencing, the horse readily participates knowing when and where the trimmer, handler, and tools/equipment are at in each of the *5 Basic Positions.* ***True. p. 98.*** **"True" can't be said enough!**

Final Notes to Student:

- From pages 107 to 143 (Chapter 9) I delineate each of the "10 distinct steps" of the natural trim. Logically, this information will remain largely an abstraction — words not rooted in practice — until your Step 2 clinic, later your Step 4 clinic, and finally, your Field Mentorships. Nevertheless, go diligently through the descriptions absorbing what you can. It is highly recommended that you study this chapter during your Step 2 clinic "off time" to draw lines between what you have read and then practiced under your clinician's guiding hand.

- Chapter 10 (pp. 144-159) concerns shoe pulling. Clinicians may or may not emphasize this in their clinics, and personally, I discourage student involvement with de-shoeing altogether. It is part of farriery, per se, not NHC. Instead, my advice is to make it your future client's responsibility to have their a farrier remove the shoes but, subsequently, not trim the hooves. But this is only my advice, and you should discuss the prospect of teaching shoe pulling with your clinician in advance of Step 2. If that is the case, then study Chapter before Step 2.

The Natural Trim

Principles and Practice

1. Until more recent centuries, the historical record shows that most horses have been ridden unshod since their domestication 8,000 or more years ago. ***True. p. 15.***

2. With the advent of the Industrial Revolution in the late 18th century, most European, and later American, horses were routinely shod. ***True. p. 17.* Arguably all of this early shoeing was crude and pretty devastating to horses and their feet. I've quoted several credible 19th Century observers to this effect in several past editions of my books.**

3. By 1900, most horse owners had no memory of the pre-horseshoeing days, such had become the convention of horseshoeing. ***True. p. 18.***

4. The "jump" to NHC did not occur overnight, however. It began rather slowly, and, admittedly, cautiously, with certain of my professional shoeing clients who seemed open-minded to the possibilities. ***True. p. 19.***

5. Interest in NHC was never confined to the United States, indeed, from the outset, it arose simultaneously in Europe, the UK, countries of the Middle East, Australia, New Zealand, Mexico, Chile, and other places. More recently, interest has come from countries once held hostage behind the Iron Curtain of Soviet control. ***True. p. 20.***

6. NHC is still relatively new to the horse-using community compared to the 800 year farrier tradition. ***True. p. 20.* I suppose the suggestion here is for NHC practitioner "patience!"**

7. Rejecting the value of "wildness" in the horse, in a sense, is foolish because it means rejecting the horse's biological roots. ***True. p. 32.***

8. Feral horses, like domesticated horses, genetically speaking, are all derived from the same wild animal, *Equus ferus ferus.* Meaning, they are still the same species. ***True. p. 32.* Can't be said enough because, by and large, this is not understood across the horse using community.**

9. The difference, then, between wild horses at the dawn of domestication upon the Eurasian steppes thousands of years ago and all horses today, is not in variant species, but in the wilderness and domesticated *experiences*. ***True. p. 34.* "Lifestyles" can also be substituted for experiences. Surprisingly, many ISNHCP students have missed this one on their quizzes.**

10. Natural selection is the process by which those heritable traits (e.g., hair color serving as camouflage or sexual attraction) that make it more likely for an organism to survive and successfully reproduce become more common in a population over successive generations. ***True. p. 34.***

11. Scientists studying the genetic evolution of the horse believe that the modern horse, *Equus ferus caballus* evolved through natural selection over a stretch of 55 million years following the extinction of the last dinosaurs in the Cretatious Pe-

riod, arriving as we know them today (based on their DNA) approximately 1.4 to 1.7 million years ago, long before the dawn of humans. *True. p. 34.* **All important information that NHC is built upon.**

12. By the time the Spanish arrived in the American southwest, the region more closely resembled the semi-arid Eurasian steppes where *Equus ferus ferus* had long ago survived, flourished, and became domesticated — at the same time members of their species perished in late-Pleistocene North America. *True. p. 35.* **This historical information is extremely significant as it demonstrates the horse's return to their adaptive environment following further changes in the earth's climate where they once again survived and flourished. From this we are able to deduce which environments favor the horse's survival with vitality and those which do not. Paddock Paradise uses this information also.**

13. As it turns out, not all wild horse or "feral" herds are suitable as models for NHC and the natural trim as they do not inhabit the high desert type *biome* (ecosystem) of their specie's ancient adaptation. *True. p. 36.* **This observation is derived from Q12.**

14. Both the Duelmener and Dartmoor horses — typically suffering from laminitis — as with many other feral horse populations in the world, are simply poor study groups for NHC practitioners due to their non-adaptive habitats. *True. p. 37.* **In fact, I was able to predict this based on Q12 above when people first brought them to my attention many years ago. Several of our AANHCP members check them out to verify.**

15. The world of NHC is built upon four inseparable and defining foundational pillars: *natural boarding, a reasonably natural diet, natural horsemanship, and the natural trim. True. p. 39.*

16. Regarding the matter of natural horsemanship . . . there is no good and reliable system of horsemanship based on our wild horse model. *True. p. 40.* **While I rest my case here, it's not that certain equestrian disciplines don't possess elements of the wild horse model, which some certainly do. It's that those I'm familiar with are not well-rounded by the other 3 Pillars. Like the natural diet of the horse, natural horsemanship has not yet risen to the level of a confirmed Pillar.**

[Note to student: From page 41 to page 48 is one of the more detailed descriptions of how the Lompoc, California Paddock Paradise was put together in 2010. So this is worth reading closely. Although it evolved over the next eight years this is the only such detailed description to date.]

17. Horse feeds should be free of sweeteners such as molasses, cane or beet sugar, sugar beet pulp, and high fructose corn syrup, as all of these have been implicated in laminitis. *True. p. 48.* **It is the position of the ISNHCP that horses are a insulin-resistant species and cannot metabolize such diets no more than the human diabetic.**

18. Avoid all grass pasture turnouts, except the natural Great Basin types foraged by wild, free-roaming horses, as these also are implicated in laminitis. *True. p. 49.*

19. There is considerable anecdotal evidence that chemical parasiticides and vaccinations may also be triggers for laminitis in horses. ***True. p. 49.*** **Those of us who have worked for many years in the field and do so as NHC practitioners have witnessed such triggered outcomes.**

20. The Mongols of East-Central Asia use horses for their transportation, as they have for thousands of years. Their horses are neither trimmed nor shod, and their hooves are exemplary by NHC standards. ***True. p. 49.*** **This has been investigated by members of the AANHCP. When a tribal elder was asked by one of our members, "What hoof care tools do you use," the response was, "Mother Nature."**

[Note to student: Chapters 3, 4, and 5 are sufficiently covered, and even updated here and there, in your other readings as to require not much more than a close reading. Having said this, one part of Chapter 5 is worth quizzing you on here as it will surface in your Final Written Exam.]

21. The "Four Guiding Principles of the Natural Trim" are based entirely on the wild horse model. Therefore, they connect us directly to the laws of nature and the powerful forces of adaptation that created the horse's foot through the evolutionary descent of *Equus ferus caballus* through natural selection. ***True. p. 86.***

22. Guiding Principle #1, "Leave that which naturally should be there," refers to the protection and preservation by the trimmer of the integrity of the basic anatomical parts of the hoof, such as the frog, bars, sole, and hoof wall. ***True. p. 86.*** **But what does this mean to you as an NHC Student?**

23. Guiding Principle #2, "Remove only that which is naturally worn away in the wild," means that when the hoof (i.e., epidermis or capsule) is reduced by the trimmer, only that which would be worn away in the horse's wild state is taken. **True. *p. 86.*** **But what else is also implied in this admonition?**

24. Guiding Principle #3, "Allow to grow that which should be there naturally but isn't due to human meddling," instructs the trimmer to use restraint when faced with hooves that have been over trimmed in some part. ***True. p. 86.*** **But what two particular violations of this admonition are being addressed relating to trimming? What violation concerns "corrective horseshoeing?"**

25. Guiding Principle #4, "Ignore all pathology," warns the trimmer not to focus on pathology (if present) or violations of the three previous principles, but, instead, to look intuitively to 4th-dimensional changes (healing changes over time — "respect the healing powers of nature") and to faithfully adhere to NHC principles and practices. ***True. p. 88.*** **But why do such an "illogical" thing as ignoring pathology, present or otherwise?**

26. The natural trim (governed by the *Four Guiding Principles*) triggers a cascade of integrated biodynamic (i.e., living) forces that produce and reinforce naturally shaped hooves. This melding of forces is sometimes described as a reinforcing "cycle of form and function." ***True. p. 88.*** **How does this cycle, in reality, define the natural trim?**

Final notes to student:

- Chapter 6 visits the *Healing Angle (H°)* and related critical measurements. Reading this entire chapter closely can't but help reinforce and clarify earlier discussions in *The Natural Horse* and the *Basic Guidelines*. Some of the discussions cross over into deformed hooves — this is material not included in this training program, but feel free to go through it with the understanding that it lays outside the scope of what you will be held accountable for.

- Chapter 7 revisits the *Hoof Mechanism*. Of interest is the presentation of conflicting viewpoints on the Mechanism. Students should take from this reading what the consequences are of adopting one over another, particularly as its theories are applied to the hoof.

- The *Introduction to Part II* of *Principles and Practice* (pages 159 to 175) concludes the required reading in this text. The section on *RD* and *support diagonals* is, to my way of thinking, very important. Especially if you don't want to get hurt working with horses, particularly with horses you don't know or know anything about, and, at that, being under such horses in close contact.

- Chapter 15 is something you can look over briefly. This is the NHC *specialized dissection* you will be taught and doing in your Step 2 Clinic.

- Chapter 16 is more on de-shoeing, but your previous reading assignment in the *Basic Guidelines* provides the same information. Review here at your discretion.

- The *Glossary* and *Index of NHC Terms* is there to help you quickly locate and review words and definitions in the text that you should know.

the Hoof Balancer

A Unique Tool For
Balancing Equine Hooves

1. The meaning of "balanced hooves" in the hoof care world is rife with unsubstantiated opinions and methods that compromise the natural integrity of the hoof and the ability of the horse to move naturally. *True. p. 4.* **There is some evidence that the farrier community has taken up the issue of "hoof balance" as direct result of NHC's influence dating to the late 1980s. However, the concept of natural balance necessarily fused with the farrier premise that shoeing, a "necessary evil," also meant providing support and protection of the hoof. Of course, one cannot naturally balanced the hoof if, by NHC definition, shoeing obstructs the necessary internal growth mechanisms that create genuine, not ersatz, naturally shaped hooves. Consequently, what we see in "balanced" shod hooves are anything but natural to the species.**

2. The *Hoof Balancer Tool* (functioning as SP) is used for two purposes: to determine the location of *active* and *passive wear* in the hoof's Volar Plane, which serve to define natural *hoof balance*; and in sighting and marking the *Mediolateral Heel Axis* (MLHA), which defines *heel balance* — an inseparable and consummating dimension of natural hoof balance. *True. p. 4.*

3. The *Hoof Balancer* can be used at any time during the course of the natural trim. *True. p. 4.*

4. The *Hoof Balancer* will require a working knowledge of three Navigational Landmarks derived from the Hoof Plexus: the MAVP, MPVP and MLHA. *True. p. 10.*

5. The groove of the *Hoof Balancer tool* is aligned with the MAVP sighted or drawn on the hoof. *True. p. 12.* **Students use this tool to develop their "eye" for sighting the hoof for natural balance without the tool. The tool will most likely be necessary with extreme capsule deformity, however.**

6. To find MLHA, the Balancer is held at the back of the hoof at an angle and then aligned with the same reference points that also define the MAVP: *cleft of the heel bulbs, central cleft (sulcus) of the frog,* and *point of frog. True. p. 13.* **To be practiced on cadaver hooves in your Step 2 Clinic.**

7. The *Mediolateral Heel Axis* (MLHA) is a single cut-line drawn across the back of both heels and the frog; it lies at a right angle (90°) to the MPVP. *True. p. 13.*

8. By definition of the *Hoof Plexus*, the MLHA is perpendicular (90°) to the SP; therefore, it is also parallel with the ground. *True. p. 13.* **Confirm in your own mind why this is true.**

9. The wild horse model dictates that the natural trim guidelines are *not* concerned with the relative locations of the heels toward or away from the MAVP. Nor are they concerned with their relative locations toward or away from the toe pillar. Finally, they are not concerned with the actual measurable lengths of

the heels from the coronary band to the SP. Instead, the guidelines are concerned only with heel length — whatever each might be — relative to the MLHA. *True. p. 14.* **Obviously, all of these statements need to be evaluated and confirmed in your own mind.**

10. Without the *Hoof Plexus*, there would be no logical way to deduce natural heel balance. *True. p. 14.* **The reason is that the complexities associated with active and passive wear in the wild horse hoof had to be worked through the Hoof Plexus. Without the wild horse hoof, everything would be left to chance and unsubstantiated opinions — which are terribly rampant across the horse using community.**

11. The upper or lower edge of the *Hoof Balancer's* window is set level with the frog after it has been trimmed to its natural size, or to where its natural length has been determined by "frog notching." *True. p. 14.* **So this presents hands-on exercises to confirm during Step 2.**

12. A black ink Sharpie is used to mark the MLHA on the back of each heel; these are the cut-lines for lowering and balancing the heels. *True. p. 14.*

13. *Active and passive wear* can be located by passing a piece of paper or thin object between the hoof wall and the *Hoof Balancer*. *True. p. 18.*

14. The frog should be level with or just passive to the *Hoof Balancer*. *True. p. 18.*

15. Placement and positioning of the *Hoof Balancer* against the back of the hoof is critical if the MLHA is to be marked correctly. *True. p. 24.* **Relates to Q15, and more hands-on exercises to confirm you can to do it.**

16. Allowing one's focus to shift above or below the Balancer's upper or lower window edge will result in a parallax shift of the MLHA. *True. p. 24.* **This potential problem is something you should be mindful of, less you generate incorrect MLHA cut-lines.**

17. Aligning the *Hoof Balancer's* grooved line to the MPVP, and then aligning one's focus on either window edge, will minimize or preclude any parallax corruption of the MLHA. *True. p. 24.* **Okay, so I've provided you with some pretty specific instructions for staying out of trouble!**

Paddock Paradise
A Guide to
Natural Horse Boarding

1. The horse naturally must be free to move constantly, and everything depends on it for his mental and physical well-being and soundness. ***True. p. 9.* This should be obvious to anyone having entered the ISNHCP Training Program.**

2. I discovered that the very lifestyle of the wild horse, driven by natural behavior, lay at the bottom of optimum hoof form and health. ***True. p. 10.* This is to remind people that the natural trim is limited and cannot "force" the horse and their hooves to be sound. There are other Pillars necessarily involved.**

3. Paddock Paradise aims to open the door to the missing freedom and lifestyle of the domesticated horse's natural world by situating and propelling the animal forward in an unprecedented environmental configuration that, holistically speaking, both stimulates and facilitates natural movement. ***True. p. 11.* This statement is a response to Q2 above.**

4. Wild horse society is comprised of family groups, never isolated individuals. ***True. p. 18.***

5. To the uninitiated human eye, one would readily conclude that band movements are random, and that the actual home range is without "boundaries" in the mind of the horse. But neither is the case at all, and, thus well-defined space and structured movement through it comprise yet another invaluable "lesson from the wild." ***True. p. 18.***

6. At the heart of the home range are one or more water holes. All band movements center around these. The tracks leading away from the water holes, sooner or later turn back to them, depending on temperature and thirst. ***True. p. 18.***

7. BLM managers in the early days of government gathers learned quickly that wild horse families "on track" do not like to leave their home ranges. ***True. p. 19.***

8. The better our picture of the wild horse's natural behaviors, the better able we will be to provide similar opportunities within Paddock Paradise. ***True. p. 19.* Because if we just do anything we please, instead of embedding the "lessons from the wild," Paddock Paradise may very well become quite something else.**

9. Wild horses at the water hole, particularly during warm months, will often roll in the dirt, if not in the water, in order to muddy-up their coats. This is "rolling behavior" and it constitutes an important lesson from the wild." ***True. p. 20.* Resulting in beautiful coats as the caked mud or dirt are shed.**

10. Grazing behavior in the wild is a slow, mouth-to-the-ground, eat-n-go affair along and near their paths. ***True. p. 21.* This is not to say that they don't stop to nibble in one area before moving on. *PP* (book) explains how we can**

achieve this on track.

11. Much of the wild horse diet appears to be range grasses and grass-like plants, and probably a wide variety of high desert type legumes. *True. p. 21.*

12. Some researchers have reported that wild horses spend roughly half their daily lives eating. *True. p. 21.*

13. In wild horse country, there are favorite sleeping areas away from perceived threats, both in open and not-so-open country where predator movement is more readily detected. *True. p. 22.* **What significance does this have in relation to PP?**

14. In the same way that thirst regulates the degree of track movement away from the water hole, so does the availability of forage and other vital nutrients, stallion rivalry, and pressure from predators, impact the speed of movement on a given track. *True. p. 23.* **All of this tallies to lives on the move.**

15. Another "lesson from the wild" is that we should make every effort to "dress up" Paddock Paradise in the simple name of natural beauty. *True. p. 25.* **Think about what this might mean to a horse.**

16. Wild horses will use their hooves to dig up vital mineral (calcium) deposits and then grind them up with their teeth . . . a way of managing their own teeth while meeting important nutritional needs. In PP, it may aid or substitute the veterinary practice of rasping the dental arcades. *True. p. 26.* **I can't recall where in our abundance of educational materials where I wrote seeing a family band eating calcium rocks such that a massive cloud of white dust nearly obscured them from being seen.**

17. Numerous theories are being presented as to what is normal tooth structure, what abnormalities are correctable, and how much correction should be done. To date, no controlled documented studies have been presented to show the benefits of aggressive rasping of the dental arcades, especially to the table surfaces of equine teeth. *True. p. 26.* **This is a direct quote — find it on this page. Very important information!**

18. Equine and bovine, and occasional mule deer and antelope, are complementary feeders and do not compete aggressively for available forage. Each "stays to its own" and go there own way. *True. p. 28.* **I witnessed very little comingling of these species.**

19. There is a subtle temptation to disperse — that is, to fan out across the alluvial plain where others can't compete for every mouthful of grass. But the "herding" instinct for self-preservation — again, the ubiquitous threat of the stealthful cougar — is too powerful to tolerate dispersion. Nor would alpha stallions allow it. *True. p. 28.* **This speaks to the powerful centrifugal and centripetal social forces I address in the book.**

20. "Mutual grooming" has an important ritualistic place in bonding between horses as well a deterrent to aberrant behavior stemming from isolation. *True. p. 32.* **Actually I'm drawing a contrast here with domesticated horses living in isolation with the result of engaging in almost ritualistic self-destructive behaviors.**

21. It may be that in Paddock Paradise, if configured closely after our wild model, horse worming may not be necessary or even desirable. *True. p. 33.*

22. Immense beds of pulverized, sharp-edged, igneous rock from these lava flows carpet large areas of wild horse country. Yet, our [wild] horses move over them effortlessly and without any apparent hypersensitivity or deleterious effect upon their feet. *True. p. 40.* **This is almost hard to believe, but in wild horse country, we hope that seeing is believing.**

23. Wild mares may form a "mares' circle" to rest and ignore the commotion of battling stallions, but also a defense formation used to protect the young when predators threaten the herd. *True. p. 44.* **I believe other wild species do this — elephants coming to mind.**

24. At the water hole, many bands converge, as though on notice to do so at the same time. As many as 100 horses may be present, each band taking turns in order of relative dominance. *True. p. 44.*

25. The water hole interaction is an important time in the sexual selection of wild horse society. Young females leave or are driven off by their fathers to find their mates. Some older stallions are unseated by a younger generation, and older mares may elect to leave with a deposed senior. Or a more aggressive or astute male will simply de-throne an aging alpha male. A myriad of possibilities. *True. p. 45.*

26. Some researchers have cited as many as 200 different legumes comprising about 10% of the bulk diet. Consistent with my own field observations is the Hansen, et al. finding that the wild horse diet is comprised mainly of grasses and sedges, although altitude and regional biomes will cause shifts in eating behavior based on availability of specific forage. What this means is that the wild horse diet is far more adaptable and complex than most of us can begin to imagine. *True. p. 45.*

27. As time went by, I began to speculate that natural wear may only arise from natural behavior, such as we see in the wild — behavior that we seldom see among domesticated horses. And to a lesser extent, from the effects of environment. *True. p. 53.*

28. The "lessons from the wild" described in Chapter 1 provide us with the essential guidelines for constructing Paddock Paradise. *True. p. 64.*

29. First, you don't need a large property for Paddock Paradise. You don't need land the size of a typical home range. In fact, the larger your property is, proportionally the less of it you will need to use! Again, it's how we use the land, not how much we own. *True. p. 64.*

30. Paddock Paradise also ignores the shape of your property, which can be any shape (or size). In fact, the final design of your Paddock Paradise will be up to you and you can adapt it to all or part of your property. *True. p. 64.*

31. In Paddock Paradise we are going to literally confine him to his "track" (with a few diversions spaced here and there), in effect preventing him from dispersing and doing nothing. Activities along the way will provide the necessary stimuli to motivate him to move along forward on track. *True. p. 66.*

32. It was my observation in wild horse country that movement based on ordinary behavior constituted about 95 percent of their locomotive energy expended; extraordinary behavior only 5 percent, or less. *True. p. 67.*

33. Paddock Paradise is the horse's home, or more precisely, his home range. I believe we should respect it as such, and, for the most part, stay out of it. *True. p.*

68.

34. My research of the wild horse diet suggests that horses will benefit from being fed a mix of grass-type hays, unsweetened oats in small quantities, mineral and salt licks, and water. Until we learn more about the horse's natural diet, I would caution horse owners from feeding much of anything else, particularly horses suffering or recovering from laminitis. *True. p. 76.* **See the current NHC recommended diet in your learning materials.**

35. What we want to do is spread the feed, particularly the hay, around the track at regulated intervals. The idea is to space the hay so that the horses will keep moving. If we place too much in one spot, or in only one location, we will encourage "camping." Camping is okay, but it shouldn't be feeding behavior based. *True. p. 77.*

36. There seem to be two distinct patterns of rolling behavior in wild horse country. One is a "mud" bath and occurs in relation to the water hole, the other occurs elsewhere on track and is more of a "dusting" experience. *True. p. 86.*

37. I believe the terrain through which the track passes should be as interesting and diverse as we can make it. If sections of your land are convoluted, if it has a stream or a pond, is wooded, rocky, whatever, direct the track into those areas. We want the horse to work his body and his feet. Flat land is okay too, but . . . " *True. p. 86.*

Laminitis
An Equine Plague Of
Unconscionable Proportions

Laminitis: A Plague Quiz Key

1. Laminitis is, in fact, an enormous profiteering racket that feeds the voracious appetite of what can only be called a "laminitis industry." ***True. p. 9.*** **This certainly is one way to look at it.**

2. Laminitis is actually an inflammatory disease of the whole horse with symptoms that erupt in many parts of the horse's body, including the feet. ***True. p. 10.***

3. Laminitis is a symptom of what I understand to be a Whole Horse Inflammatory Disease (WHID). ***True. p. 11.*** **Pointing to WHID "officially" redefines laminitis in the world of NHC.**

4. Technically, laminitis is the pathological separation of the hoof from the horse, one of many symptoms of WHID. ***True. p. 11.***

5. The conventional definition of laminitis used most often by veterinarians, farriers and barefoot trimmers, and horse owners who've had to deal with it, is *inflammation of the (dermal) lamina*, hence the term *laminitis*. ***True. p. 11.***

6. *Lamina* refers to the network of dermal and epidermal leaf-like structures that interlock together to form a complex bridge of connective tissue between the inner hoof wall and the outer face of the lowermost bone of the horse's foot, called the coffin bone — known variously as the pedal bone, distal phalanx, and P3. ***True. p. 11.***

7. The body of a dermal leaf is comprised of fibrous connective tissue, and is both vascular (contains blood) and innervated (contains nerves). ***True. p. 12.***

8. *The* epidermal leaves, in contrast to the dermal leaves, are also fibrous, but are neither enervated nor vascular. ***True. p. 12-13.***

9. The dermal and epidermal leaves are connect together to form the Lamellar Attachment Mechanism, or "LAM." ***True. p. 13.***

10. Not visible to the naked eye, is another component of each dermal leaf called the *basal* or *basement membrane*. This is a thin membranous layer of connective tissue that covers the underlying vascular tissue of the dermal leaf. ***True. p. 13.*** **More specifically, it coats the outer surface of the SDLs, although they are mere extensions of the PDLs.**

11. Epithelial cells continuously proliferate from the basement membrane to form the *secondary epidermal leaves (lamina)*, or SELs. As each SEL is produced, it adheres to the "host" PEL through cellular migration and integration. ***True. p. 13.*** **Although veterinary researchers have looked closely at laminitis pathophysiology, missing are NHC healing pathways that raise new questions about SEL behavior.**

12. Through the actions of specialized enzymes operative in the environment (called proteolysis), the cellular bonds between the PELs and SELs are cleaved

and replaced by new generations of proliferating epithelial cells. In this way, the hoof wall (including the attached PELs) is detached and able to grow down past the stationary SELs, basement membrane and the underlying connective tissue of the dermal leaves, to which P3 is attached. *True. p. 14.*

13. Laminitis is set off in the lower intestine by substances consumed (sweet feeds, medications, supplements, etc.) or injected medications such as antibiotics, sedatives, pain killers, steroids, vaccinations, etc.) that favor the proliferation of harmful hind gut bacteria. *True. p. 14.* **This statement brings us back to WHID and NHC practitioners are advised not to let down their understanding of this. Horse owners are deluged with information that keeps them glued to the hoof as the focus of the problem.**

14. Hind gut bacterial contamination impact enzymes naturally present in the LAM responsible for breaking down the epithelial cells so that the hoof can naturally descend past P3. These enzymes now proliferate pathologically, destroying the cellular bonds that are responsible for securing the wall to P3 and faster than normal mechanisms involved can repair them. *True. p. 16.*

15. If proteolysis is not halted by appropriate changes in the horse's diet, the LAM will continue to degrade and eventually become a tangled mass of disorganized growth. *True. p. 16.* **To be clear, I'm addressing proteolysis that is out of control.**

16. Degradation of the LAM is accompanied by inflammatory symptoms within the foot, particularly during acute attacks; these may include severe pain, elevated temperatures, and a palpable pounding pulse above the coronary band. *True. p. 16.* **All of this should be part of your repertoire of understanding.**

17. Ignoring causality and nature's healing pathways, conventional care has resulted in treatment strategies that are typically and unnecessarily mechanical, invasive, ineffective, and worse, damaging not only to the foot, but to the horse's overall well-being. *True. p. 18.* **Farriers, concerned principally with moving steel around on the horse's hoof, and the vet, concerned with treating symptoms, facilitate laminitis by ignoring WHID.**

18. Treating laminitis as though it originates or is limited to the foot is an invitation to disaster. *True. p. 19.*

19. "Cresty necks," obesity, psychological distress, hives, itchy skin, appearing to be arthritic, and other types of lameness are all symptomatic of laminitic horses, but also of WHID. *True. p. 19.* **The message here is, as NHC practitioners, to stop thinking in terms of "laminitis" and taking action on WHID, the main battleground for healing.**

20. Stated simply, laminitis *triggers* are any substances, natural or artificial, that distress the horse's metabolic processes resulting in laminitis. *True. p. 20.*

21. Sugars in all forms are triggers, yet many horse feeds include significant amounts of molasses, sugar beet pulp, and/or cane sugar. *True. p. 20.*

22. Artificial triggers are those biological, chemical, and agricultural products manufactured by the laminitis industry. *True. p. 20.*

23. In short, while there are many possible laminitis triggers, not all horses may react the same to them. *At least in the short term. True. p. 21.*

24. Treating and presenting laminitis works like this: *known* triggers are removed entirely (or mostly so) from the horse's lifestyle, and the horse is then brought into the broad, holistic fold of NHC based on the wild horse model. *True. p. 22.* **In fact, it is advisable to start here before doing anything at the hoof. If the horse's owner won't cooperate, work at the hoof is an exercise in futility — arguably becoming complicit in the animal's suffering.**

25. Laminitis pathophysiology occurs in three stages of progressive development: *sub-clinical (absence of pain)* → *clinical (observable pain)* → *chronic (sub-clinical + clinical).* *True. p. 23.* **This is largely if not entirely unknown by horse owners, farriers, and even vets, the result of not understanding the pathogenesis of laminitis in WHID.**

26. The *sub-clinical stage* of laminitis is characterized by no observable pain. *True. p. 23.*

27. The *clinical stage* of laminitis is characterized by observable pain, obstruction of the natural gaits, and other overt changes in the horse's body, demeanor and metabolic processes. *True. p. 27.* **Of concern here is that horse owners, under the direction of vets, conceal the pain with drugs.**

28. Symptoms of the *chronic stage of* laminitis tend to be off and on, and may include any of the previous symptoms (sub-clinical and clinical) plus a range of possible hoof deformities, aberrant upper body hair growth, dysfunctional internal organs, inability to move naturally, and neurotic psychological distress. *True. p. 27.*

29. Founder, technically, is a consequence of laminitis. The term is often used synonymously with laminitis, but there is a difference. Specifically, founder means that the lowermost bone of the horse's foot has separated from the hoof wall due to a catastrophic failure of the LAM. *True. p. 36.* **Actually, there is a much larger discussion here, but it belongs in the *Advanced Guidelines.***

[Study note to student: From Chapter 6 until the end of the book, the primary focus is on rehabilitative efforts to help the laminitic horse. While these are important chapters to study at this point in your training, they are arguably best understood in the context of your field training (i.e., the Field Mentorships), when you will undoubted begin to run into laminitic horses suffering minor deformity. Remember, the thrust of your education focuses on the *Basic Guidelines* of the natural trim — not the *Advanced Guidelines.* The Basic natural trim needs to be mastered before venturing into laminitis pathology. So, in these chapters, approach them from the standpoint of humane management protocols (4 Pillars of NHC) based on the wild horse model, rather than what you think you can glean from them to trim laminitic horses. For this reason, there are no trimming instructions in this book.]

Image Credits

Index

About the Author

Jaime Jackson is an ISNHCP Clinician and a professional hoof care provider since the 1970s. The ISNHCP Natural Trim Training Program is based on Jackson's research of wild, free-roaming horses living in the U.S. Great Basin.

www.ingramcontent.com/pod-product-compliance
Lightning Source LLC
Chambersburg PA
CBHW080628030426
42336CB00018B/3119